SINÉAD O'CONNOR

SINÉAD O'CONNOR
THE LAST INTERVIEW
and OTHER CONVERSATIONS

with an introduction by KRISTIN HERSH

MELVILLEHOUSE
BROOKLYN · LONDON

SINÉAD O'CONNOR: THE LAST INTERVIEW
AND OTHER CONVERSATIONS

Copyright © 2024 by Melville House Publishing

Introduction © 2024 by Kristin Hersh

"Somebody Up There Likes Me": From "Girls at the greasy
end of the rock business" © 1986 by Kate Holmquist.
Reprinted with permission from *The Irish Times*.

"I Open My Mouth and Scream" © NME 1988

"Sinéad O'Connor: The *Rolling Stone* Interview" © 1991 by David Wild

"Special Child" © 1991 by Bob Guccione, Jr., founder of *SPIN*

"Going It Alone" © 2004 by Deirdre Mulrooney

"Jah Nuh Dead" © 2004 by Nicholas Jennings

"Something Beautiful" © 2007 by Jody Denberg

"How About I Be Me (and You Be You?" © 2014 by Chris Azzopardi.
Reprinted with permission from *Pride Source*.

"Protest Singer" © 2021 Courtesy of ABCNEWS VIDEOSOURCE

First Melville House printing: December 2024

Melville House Publishing   Suite 2000
        46 John Street   and   16/18 Woodford Road
Brooklyn, NY 11201   London E7 0HA

mhpbooks.com
@melvillehouse

ISBN: 978-1-68589-185-5
ISBN: 978-1-68589-186-2 (EBOOK)

Printed in the United States of America
1   3   5   7   9   10   8   6   4   2

A catalog record for this book is available from the Library of Congress.

CONTENTS

vii   **INTRODUCTION**
Kristin Hersh
New Orleans, May 2024

3   **SOMEBODY UP THERE LIKES ME**
Interview by Kate Holmquist
The Irish Times
October 17, 1986

9   **I OPEN MY MOUTH AND SCREAM**
Interview by Barry Egan
NME
October 29, 1988

23   **THE *ROLLING STONE* INTERVIEW**
David Wild
March 7, 1991

45   **SPECIAL CHILD**
Interview by Bob Guccione, Jr.
SPIN
November 1991

85   **GOING IT ALONE**
Interview by Deirdre Mulrooney
"Mothers and Babies" supplement,
The Irish Independent
July 2004

93   **JAH NUH DEAD**
Interview by Nicholas Jennings
Inside Entertainment
July 2005

111   **SOMETHING BEAUTIFUL**
Interview by Jody Denberg
KUTX 98.9 Radio, Austin, Texas
April 11, 2007

133   **HOW ABOUT I BE ME (AND YOU BE YOU)?**
Interview by Chris Azzopardi
Pride Source
July 22, 2014

145   **THE LAST INTERVIEW: PROTEST SINGER**
The View
American Broadcasting Company
June 25, 2021

INTRODUCTION

KRISTIN HERSH

In 2005, Sinéad O'Connor and I sat in a dressing room in London together, people watching and listening, eyeing the music biz swirl around us suspiciously. Neither of us was familiar with the other's work, which helped us to speak freely; unattached to anything but a shared impression of humanity we both needed to help us with our stage fright.

It was an uncomfortable night, not *our* show, not a show with which we were familiar; so we were jittery, hoping to be allowed to leave soon. In that moment, we were two *people* though—not two performers—and we chatted like women on a bus. I didn't know her music because pop stars weren't interesting to me, so I didn't pay attention to them, and she didn't know *my* music because nobody *but* pop stars are interesting to normal people. And she was a pretty normal person, I think, though she'd been accused of strangeness, of craziness, as had I. It's like somebody somewhere had decided that, having broken too many rules, we fit in no category, and so we were not invited to the party. Having been invited once and met with anger, she felt alienated. Having never cared about the party, so did I, when I learned that it was the only game in town. Alienation helps with clarity, though, as it adds the objectivity of no longer swimming in those waters.

Alienation was only one of the things we had in common: we were also mothers, having had babies and released our first records about the same time, in the late eighties, when we were very young. We were both shy, both outspoken, and we both had resting fear face. And clearly, we were of a different ilk than the rock stars milling around us. I want to say that we were without display, and in that company this quality was very apparent.

She wasn't allowed to smoke in the dressing room because there were so many vocalists back there, and that was driving her nuts.

"Want some gum?" I asked her as I started fishing around in my backpack for some Dentyne that was at least a couple of years old. I found it and unwrapped a gooey piece for her, which she accepted carefully. "It's . . . old," I told her. "You don't have to eat it."

Dozens of people talked, laughed, dressed, undressed, fussed, and drank around us, while we sat on a small, discarded riser, watching. There was some jockeying for position status-wise for us to watch, and some bonding. Some *don't-touch-me-I'm-famous*, some *please-love-me-I'm a-freak*. Typical dressing room stuff.

"Where do they learn to do that?" She put the gum in her mouth and nodded toward an entourage actively worshipping the star in the center of their commotion. The group radiated a strange energy: buzzing and alert, they focused on the star while appearing to deflect stranger danger, keeping people away. It looked like a kind of cellular patterning.

"Yeah." I watched the huddle jealously guard its nucleus. "Some people learn the narcissist side of the equation and some learn the sycophant side. But it's the same equation."

She touched her fingers to her face in a V shape as if they held a cigarette. "Do they even *like* each other?"

"I don't know. They seem kind of angry." The entourage made its way across the room, through other entourages, past bowls of fruit and bottles of wine, and then disappeared through a door on the other side—still buzzing, still deflecting. "What do *you* think?"

Chewing my terrible Dentyne, she squinted at the door closing behind the group. "I think . . . that the people who treated me like that were the same ones who ended up hating me."

I looked at her, struck by this. "Hating you?" She nodded, distracted, and I shook my head. "I'm sorry."

"It's because I don't keep my mouth shut."

"Oh." We watched a line of people applying makeup in mirrors, their faces surrounded by hot yellow light bulbs. "Why should you keep your mouth shut? What do you say?"

"All kindsa stuff. Stuff I believe." Staring, blank eyed, she looked stricken. "Didn't know you weren't supposed to do that."

I shrugged. "Maybe *they* aren't supposed to do that. If it's stuff you believe . . . seems important to say it. Some people don't believe in anything. You're lucky you care."

She looked at me. "Do *you?*"

"Care?" She just kept staring, so I kept talking. "I guess, but nobody seems to know what I'm talking about, so . . . they don't take offense."

"Offense," she repeated, laughing. "That's what I do. I offend."

"You're offensive?"

"Indeed." She told me a few stories then, relayed a few troubled moments. The seismic activity of a career in the entertainment industry that you can read about in this book. Maybe ups and downs but more like back-and-forths. Not much of what she said had anything to do with music—more sociocultural, sociopolitical. But she took it all very personally, had never left that almost childlike view, surprised that attracting attention could attract negative attention. Then she muttered something I didn't get. Something about God.

"God?"

"I always end up there," she smirked. "Freaks people out."

I nodded. "Yeah, God'll do that." I unwrapped a sticky piece of gum for myself. "But we could use more God here. Maybe choose a different word next time."

Sinéad laughed loudly, and a couple of people with lipstick and hairbrushes in their hands turned around to see what was funny, smiled at us, then turned back to their reflections. "Life?" she asked.

"Life," I agreed. "Can't play music without life." Speakers on the wall crackled, then beeped, and a voice announced that it was ten minutes until doors—meaning that the audience would soon murmur their way in, find seats, and demand that we all turn sound check into a show together. "Musicians forget that."

"I'm not a musician," she announced flatly.

"Oh," I shrugged, feeling suddenly awkward. "Well, you're *alive*."

She took the lousy gum out of her mouth. "I honestly don't know why sometimes." Getting up to wander the room looking for a wastebasket, she muttered, "I'm a mess."

This is when I realized we were on different sides of something—something I'm only now beginning to understand. My life was private, hers public. She was in light, and I was in shadow. I believed in something she didn't, and she believed in something *I* didn't—our orientations were completely opposed—and I felt for her. The illusory world of attention was equally positive and negative for her, and that caused her a lot of pain. Its bullying was real in her psychology, so she couldn't walk away from it. And yet she knew something was wrong and railed against the wrongness in that sphere, which set the bullies on a fire that they then set on her. And I could see it eating away at yet another human being—another whole person feeling subject to fake love and real hatred instead of focusing only on music.

"I don't think . . ." I tried to find the words that would help and not hurt—not hurt this person I'd known for less than an hour. "I don't think we can *solve* these problems. We can wake up and champion underdogs, but people are gonna get pissed. That's just what happens."

Sinéad looked thoughtful.

"Sorry, wait." I spat the awful gum into my palm. "That means drunk here, right? I meant pissed *off.* Where's the trash?"

"I knew what you meant." She pointed to a wastebasket between two of the mirror people. "And we just keep fighting?"

I tossed my gum between a couple of knees as the speakers crackled again, then beeped, then told us that doors were five minutes away. "Sure. Maybe we can't call it that. Sounds mad." Music from the venue began playing through the speakers. Gentle stuff. "Wait. That means *crazy* here, right? I meant angry."

"I knew what you meant."

"We keep helping?" I tried. "Can we call it *helping?*"

"Don't say *God*, don't say *fight*," she snickered.

"Say *life*, say *help*." I smiled. "Problem solved."

She sighed deeply. "All problems solved."

"Except you still can't smoke. And this gum is very terrible."

We fell back into staring; her resting fear face returned, and mine probably did too. Though my expression was not a life orientation, more of a life *irritation*, because I knew that truth would return along with real life when I was allowed to walk away from the party. Sinéad seemed to live in a corner of the party, though: believing in its troubles and causing trouble about it. What a thing for a soul to be tasked with. She seemed upset and flailing, but only because she straddled love and illusion, which was a hell of a sacrifice on her part.

I know more about her life and output now, having read these interviews: from the late Kate Holmquist's lovely consideration in *The Irish Times* of the importance of making garage music in "nowheresville"—an early career kick-start that ultimately gave Sinéad a place on the world stage—to her 2005 quote for Nicholas Jennings ("I'm interested in rescuing God from religion through music"). That one stuck with me, as she has so firmly stated that God is missing in the West, driving her own search for spiritual understanding elsewhere; one that might have helped calm her heart, ease her pain.

But her essence was more vivid to me in that dressing room than in any interview, to be honest. In the person she was, not the persona. "Lost," I want to say, but carrying the conviction that the lost may be found and could lead other souls to that *fight* for *God, helping* them toward *life*. The "troubled" card is too easy to play in retrospect; after a life has ended, we have the honor of looking back on its beauty, and we should rise to that occasion. Where is the beauty on that path?

That day and the day she died, I wished for Sinéad's sake that she could have lived a life free of judgment: privacy over publicity. In my subculture, for example, a shaved head and combat boots were *conforming*; her presentation would have incited no reaction. That would just leave her music. Humans have a long, respected history of pulling down corruption and sexism, as long as you're *outside* of—above and beneath—the superficial. That's also where music lies. I wished that she had been rewarded for depth, not breadth. Again: just the music. God *is* missing; she was right. So, find God in music and *believe* it. We would all have benefited. A true singer's power is in their body. These bodies that take the ride with us, she had one and was so willing to share its ride.

I wished she could have shouted all that she believed and made only friends, no enemies. I wished that she had never accepted that invitation to the entertainment industry party and, instead, had kept the richness of her own life untainted. I wished that she could have loved herself and everyone else. I wished that she had absorbed the spiritual peace she fought for. But that wouldn't have been Sinéad, I guess.

So where is the beauty? In all of it: in the pain, the joy, the mess, the person, and her music.

SINÉAD O'CONNOR

SOMEBODY UP THERE LIKES ME

INTERVIEW BY KATE HOLMQUIST
THE IRISH TIMES
OCTOBER 17, 1986

The garage band—it's a phrase that captures the intense, homegrown yearning of young aspiring musicians who want to be recognised by the 1980s music culture they identify with. Playing music in the "garage," in nowheresville, forming a sound, an image, working towards playing in small clubs, recording a demo tape, are part of a lifestyle that few Irish women were part of until recently.

Ireland has produced the two most compelling international figures in 1980s rock culture, Bono of U2 and Bob Geldof. But an Irish woman is yet to make a similar impact. From total anonymity to successful self-employment in the high-profile music business—It's a new kind of Cinderella story for both young Irish men and women. And Prince Charming is a record-company executive with a recording contract up his sleeve who says, "Come out of the garage and into the limelight."

Sinéad O'Connor (nineteen), who leads her own band, SINÉAD, really isn't a garage girl anymore. She has just recorded a single with the Edge, of U2, and her first album will be released in January on Ensign Records. She lives in her own apartment in London and looks back on the day she "did a bunk," at seventeen, ran away from Newtown

School in Waterford, disappeared into Dún Laoghaire and embarked on her life, with not a little satisfaction. (After all, look what happened.)

Skinhead hairstyle, sweet Laura Ashley dress, aggressive Doc Martens boots, round innocent-looking eyes and all, she says, "I'm a real schizophrenic . . . I like to contrast five or six elements of one person in me . . . I have a skinhead, but I'm not a skinhead. I have the haircut because it makes me feel clear; it makes me feel good. I like to say, 'I'm not a man or a woman—I'm Sinéad O'Connor.'"

She didn't need a fairy godmother to help her form the personal style that makes her a potential star. It all started when the headmaster at Newtown let her do a demo tape with her Irish teacher, Gerald Falvey, and a friend, Jeremy Maber. Next, she says, "I decided I wanted to be a singer."

She sang with a couple of Dublin bands (including In Tua Nua) and at one point a record-company executive, Nigel Grainge, heard her and kept in touch, suggesting that she make a tape of her own songs. Sinéad is somewhat starry-eyed and breathless in the way she describes her next break, the offer of a contract in 1985: "It was surprising. I was just kind of having a laugh. I wasn't looking for a record deal—somebody up there likes me."

Meanwhile Ossie Kilkenny, U2's accountant, heard about her contract and did his own little bit of fairy godmothering, contacting her father, a barrister, and "being very helpful in making sure it was safe for me to go ahead." Kilkenny also introduced her to Bono of U2, and the two sat down and had "a long talk" and seemed to share similar views.

"A voice is something that comes from your heart, your soul, your head and your body," says Sinéad. "I don't need to drink or take drugs. All I need to do is sing . . . It makes me feel so relieved . . . I don't want to look like a fashion model, I want to look like Sinéad. I don't wear makeup at all, I don't feel pretty—I feel like me." But she hasn't felt influenced by feminism. "It's just my personality."

I OPEN MY MOUTH AND SCREAM

INTERVIEW BY BARRY EGAN
NME
OCTOBER 29, 1988

Sinéad O'Connor has a "shaved head, real horrible legs, a big nose," and an even bigger mouth! In New York to record with self-abuse queen Karen Finley, she lays into Whitney Houston, Michael Jackson, U2, SAW [Stock Aitken Waterman], the British government and any other poor bugger who crosses her mind.

So tell me, Sinéad, what do you look like?
"Shaved head. Small. Thin. Not very thin though. I've got really, real horrible legs and a big nose."
The first thing you notice about Sinéad O'Connor—the ET cut of her coiffure—is the last thing you remember about her. An open-throated Elizabeth Fraser drunk on altar wine, she harnesses blown-in-off-the-moors atmospheric and AR Kane intensity to get you onto her side. And it works.
One of pop's Condor moments, "Troy"—the center-piece of the album that followed, *The Lion and the Cobra*—was the first signal we received that a new star was in the firmament. That it was altogether bizarre was doubtless. An exacting, almost metaphysical cut to it . . . layer upon layer of choral cloudbursts piled atop an eerie, disquieting voice. It gave Edith Piaf goose pimples and left a trail of bloated adjectives in its wake. You had to stop whatever you were doing

and listen. A terrible beauty was born and it had nothing to do with exploding planets or sad-hearted colleens . . .

"If you give somebody an album made by an Irish artist, especially in England and America, they will automatically listen to it. They will prick up their ears because they have this romanticised image of Ireland: Irish women are these great mystical women that have had all sorts of blows struck to them by life and fate, and the men are rogues and they drink a lot and all that stuff.

"They have these huge, romanticised ideas of Ireland— which is a place most people have never been to. I know loads of people who've played my records to people who've never seen me before and they always say, 'She's very small, she wears Laura Ashley dresses and she has dark black hair,' because I'm Irish, and that's what they think Irish women look like.

"The media like the idea of artists being fucked-up, angst-ridden, drug-crazy, depressed people. They don't like normal people; they can't relate to it . . . My childhood was not any more 'scarred' than a lot of people's. In fact, it was nothing compared to most people in Ireland."

Sometimes success, ephemeral or otherwise, comes to those who *don't ask* (Sinéad for once kept her mouth shut). You had her pegged for perennial cult status—Danielle Dax out of Glenageary—when the young woman with the moondust in her larynx upped and had a big-time hit with "Mand-inka": clankering, clattering power pop. That it gate-crashed the Brit chart pleasantly bamboozled Chrysalis, her record company. The singer was wholeheartedly "amused" and sure the next time she would see the number seventeen was when her baby Jake reached that birthday.

Chrysalis do not, however, seem to be holding their breath for "Mandinka II" to come hither. "I don't think they ever saw me as being a hit-making artist in the first place," Sinéad says. "It was a complete shock to them, to me and to everyone involved, when it was a hit. And I don't think the same is expected again. It was never expected in the first place.

"It's automatically understood that there's a certain way I like to do things and they don't intrude. Chrysalis America are different because they're crazy. They play very much on the aspect of how I look and I'm real *wild*! Which is shite."

Despite the out-o'-the-blue till-rattle of "Mandinka," Sinéad is a star without hits to her name, which suits her fine. Her *raison d'être*—to make music how she sees fit—has never included performing last on *Top of the Pops* or the touching of [radio and television presenter] Terry Wogan's knee, and her career to date bears witness to this.

Eschewing stagnant modes O'Connor has, instead, mined an adventurous seam: working with the people she admires and, admirably, releasing songs that certainly won't bring her within fondling distance of Terence [Wogan]'s disjointed kneecaps. Her collaboration with Queens-born rapper MC Lyte is a case in point. Clipping guitars and holocaustic bass lineage offset by Lyte's granite-tuff vocal, the S-Funk of "I Want Your (Hands on Me)" received no airplay to speak of and belly flopped.

A mooted project is a linkup with one of Anthrax's methadone-blasted axmen. The mind does tend to boggle but for now, Sinéad is in New York mixin' up the medicine with Karen Finley (an erudite ex-bartender whose records are banned in Britain and who was all but deported by [Scotland] Yard two years ago) for the twelve-inch of the new single, "Jump in the River." Complete with yowling last heard in *The Exorcist* and radio-unfriendly lyrics aplenty, the ferocity of Karen's piece is bound to get up all the right nostrils.

"I was thinking about the jump in the river bit. So I decided to do something on jump—which psychologically made me think of jump-start, you know, *get me started!*" Karen, long and gangly, hoots. "The cow bit came from a piece that I was doing about Freudian analysis and the whole idea of womb envy. I thought of a man being envious of the fact that a woman has the ability to have a child, and also have a child that loves the mother unquestionably. Whereas the father has to earn the love." Radio 1 will love it.

In a studio embedded in the underbelly of Broadway, the playback of "Jump in the River" is baton charging from the Empire State Building–sized speakers. The noise of feedback-lashed guitars colliding headlong with a sparse, slowly unfurling rhythm clears the NYC smog clean out of your ears. Outside, high-rise grotesquerie jut out en masse into the clouds and the sky is *not* the limit.

Inside, the same restriction applies. In her white "First Priority Music" jacket and her little maggot-in-tights legs with Doc Martens at the end, the twenty-one-year-old has a smile wider than the budget deficit. Her guts are telling her: *hit or not, this is hot.* Karen Finley would seem to agree. Jolting across the floor, all flailing arms, she yelps, "This would be a great record to bartend to!"

"The idea to get Karen to do the record came into my head about a week ago," Sinéad admits, whizzin' over the wooden floor of the studio booth encased in roller skates! "And that is the way that I like to do things: just get an idea and do it. I'm not concerned with—like, this single won't get played. The next single after this, which is going to be 'The Value of Ignorance,' won't get played. But I don't care, because it's a fucking good song—so I want it to be released."

I suggest why not offer the twelve-inch of "Jump in the River" to the pop kids as a single.

"Because there would be no chance of it getting played or no chance of anything happening with it at all. It wouldn't even get played in the clubs."

But if it doesn't matter to you . . .?

"But it matters to the point where the record company will not bother to try and support something that I blatantly and deliberately do so it won't get played. I have to give them a little bit.

"Chrysalis were fine about me working with Karen Finley because they know it's not going to be the seven-inch. The seven-inch will get played—so they think: OK, that will be a hit so go and do the twelve-inch how you like. They never market twelve-inches—they never marketed 'Jake's Remix' of 'Mandinka'—they just put it out. Just fuck them—I don't care. When 'The Value of Ignorance,' for example, comes out, I won't ask them to give me money to make a video for it because there is no point. I know it won't get played. There's no point in them trying to market it."

There is no room for half measures in the Sinéad psyche. That she is so diabolically passionate about "The Value of Ignorance" seeing the light of day is a testament to that and says more than I can here. And remember, Sinéad O'Connor is not on Alternative Tentacles or Self Immolation Records; she's, by the very size of her popularity, part of the mainstream. She is what amounts to an oasis in a slag heap of money-mad homogeneity.

"It's quite a vicious song and a lot of people will think I wrote it to be shocking. But I didn't. In my mind, it's about violence, mental violence of the emotional and sexual kind. Not physical violence but a type of violence that is very difficult to describe, but that is very, very intense and that can be inflicted by men on women, and can destroy them . . . The chorus is: 'All those nights with my arse in your face / And your words in my dreams / Now I know what the value of ignorance means.'

"There you go!" she half laughs, an emergent blush making a beeline across her face. "I think it's self-explanatory really. But I didn't write it in order to say a rude word like *arse*. I wrote it because it's a violent thing and it should be spoken about violently. It shouldn't be spoken about with an acoustic guitar and a soft voice."

How long before both you and your music become assimilated into the fabric of Britpop, Sinéad?

"I hope I don't. But I don't think I ever will because I don't . . . I could be now if I wanted to be.

"It's absolutely disgusting. The most despicable thing is its blatant, complete and utter racism, and its exploitation of women. Like all these people going on about the Great

Advent of Women, which is shite. They've been there all the time, it's just that record companies have decided to turn round and exploit women because—they've run out of people to exploit! Disgusting!

"And Stock Aitken and Waterman! Pete Waterman was asked how he felt about the problems in South Africa— 'What problems?' he said. *Shoot the bastard!* I would like him to be in the Hippodrome when I firebomb it."

Likewise Channel Zero's self-created porch n—s . . .

"I like Michael Jackson's music and I intrinsically like him—but it fucking disgusts me to see people like him and Whitney Houston make themselves white so that MTV will play their videos!!! MTV won't play Black artists. They won't play hard-core Black stuff. They won't play, in fact, a video by a Black artist unless it's in black and white or the artist looks white. Which is why Whitney Houston sells out. When she's asked how she feels about Black politics, she says, 'Ooh, I don't want to talk about politics. I don't care about that stuff, I just care about music.'"

While the world's media were blitzkrieging the Mandela knees-up at Wembley, Sinéad was playing a low-key birthday celebration for The Man in Dublin. There was no fuss made. A few Pogues turned up. The odd Dubliner and Christy Moore came too. And you got the feeling that, deep down, certain bands at the Wembley affair couldn't give two hoots about Mandela's jailhouse blues nor P W's institutional insanity. *"How many did you say would be watching ?!!"*

"At the Mandela thing, when they showed shots of the crowd, there were hardly any Black people there," Sinéad says.

"More people benefited directly out of the Mandela birthday celebration than Nelson Mandela! I think a lot of people do that because it makes them feel important, it elevates them in their own minds and that's why they do it. It's trendy and everything but they don't know what's really going on."

Would you have played?

The answer is violently dispatched like a javelin out of the hands of [Olympic athlete] Daley Thompson. "*No I would not!* I wouldn't step on a stage with Simple Minds or Bruce Springsteen or any of those people—no way! Nor would I do an Amnesty International tour because they don't acknowledge that there are any political prisoners in Ireland."

Talk to her of that British-created Hell-on-Earth at the top of the green and pleasant land of Ireland and she will not lose the garrulous polemic. If Sinéad had kept schtum now, her earlier maxims might as well have come from the saccharine lips of Whitney Houston.

"The British troops should be withdrawn from Northern Ireland," she states. "I don't think the British people should leave; it's as much their right to live there as anywhere else. But the fucking government should get out—and they should get their fucking death squads out with them!

"They walked up to one of the people when he was lying on the ground and shot him—four times in the head . . . you know what I mean?" Sinéad O'Connor asks passionately, and it's hard not to. "Those people were not armed. I don't like what the IRA do; I don't agree with it but I sympathise with it. *I have to sympathise with it.* If I really look in my heart and think about it, I have to sympathise. I think it's horrible and I'm really frightened by even the fact that that is how I feel, because it's a frightening thing. But what can I do—they walked up to some guy and shot him in the head four times . . ."

Let me tell you a story. Sinéad was young and innocent, as children are, and was watching the telly one night. The news came on. Some atrocity or other flashed across the cathode tube; it was terrible stuff. They caught the human being responsible but as far as young Sinéad O'Connor was concerned, if that person came on the telly and said he didn't do it—*he didn't*. It could have been a little mustachioed Austrian man. As far as she was concerned everybody was how they seemed . . .

That's all changed now. Not too many moons ago Sinéad was expecting Jake. Bono used to call round to her flat frequently with presents and what have you. He couldn't be nicer. The Edge's wife—having had two babies of her own—was also very good to the nervous, expectant mother.

Then, whilst still liking them, for the most part, as friends, Sinéad made relatively innocuous remarks to *i-D* magazine; expressing distaste for the bigness of the U2 soundscape.

That was her only sin. In a manner most unbecoming of the whole U2 sales pitch, Sinéad was ostracized. They didn't want to know her. Backstage at Wembley last year, she truly found out that people are *not* always as they seem . . .

"I went to talk to somebody and U2's accountant, Ossie Kilkenny, who was in a group of people, shouted at me that I had no right to be there, considering the things I had said, because I had said 'abusive things about people who have helped me.' Presumably they meant they had helped me by

fucking honouring me with having done the song! 'Heroine.'
And he screamed this at me in front of a whole load of people!

"Bono, who used to call round and be real friendly, completely ignored me. So I went up to him and said, 'Listen, I
don't have to like your music and all that stuff.' The reason I
said that is because I'm pissed off with the way they treated
Fachtna (O'Ceallaigh, early manager), Terry O'Neill (Pogues'
and Hothouse Flowers' Irish publicist and Real Wild West's
manager), The Real Wild West themselves and all those people associated with Mother Records.

"I said I was particularly pissed off because of the way
they treated Fachtna. They had someone employed in his
place before he was even told he was fired! They have this
big thing about helping people, in fact all they do is hinder
bands! Like The Real Wild West's tapes are still sitting in
Windmill Lane [Recording Studios]. They can't get out because U2 won't release them! How is that helping The Real
Wild West?

"U2 are not the way they seem at all. I can show you a
letter from their solicitor when I did 'Heroine' with The Edge.
They refused to pay me any money for doing it! U2 listed
eight reasons why they didn't think I should have money. The
seventh reason is that they saw the project as a fucking help
to me! I said to The Edge 'this is not happening' and he said
he didn't even know it was going on!

"He said he would personally organise I get paid. In fact,
he paid me more than I wanted 'cause he felt it was a really
shitty thing for them to have done. They've all these people
who act on their behalf without even consulting them. I've
said that to Bono and he denies it.

"They have fingers in every pie—they fucking rule Dublin. There's not a band in Dublin who could get anywhere if they weren't in some way associated with U2."

The disorientating, pistol-whip beats of a million hip-hop records was the soundtrack of my five days in America with Sinéad. Dancing to it in the sleepless clubs of New York and watching it performed in a fun park in New Jersey, it was everywhere we roamed. Public Enemy, Ice-T, KRS-One, Roxanne Shanté, Shinehead, all followed us to Washington. "It's the viciousness and the hardness of it that I love," she says. "And that it's immediately reflective of life for the people that do it. And the music, if that's what you want to call it, in the charts doesn't reflect anything. It's bilge."

What does Sinéad O'Connor's music reflect?

"Nothing," she says gratuitously. "No, how can I explain it? I would like to have a message as such, I would like to be hard-core and write these great songs but I don't. Therefore I think those people are better than me. My songs are not reflective of life on the streets of x amount of people, politically, emotionally—they're reflective of life in my head, in my own heart but not anyone else's . . ."

With unshakeable conviction, Sinéad threatens me with a promise of fierce things to come.

"My next album will be fucking vicious. Because I feel vicious. I like the viciousness of singing; I like the fact that I can stand at a microphone and scream something really vicious! I like the idea of being able to wipe the floor with people because I open my mouth and scream. It's like 'Fuck you!'"

THE *ROLLING STONE* INTERVIEW

DAVID WILD
ROLLING STONE
MARCH 7, 1991

Sinéad O'Connor really *does* want what she hasn't got.

At least it seems that way as she spends part of a sunny winter afternoon shopping at Book Soup, a popular store on Sunset Boulevard, in Hollywood. She wants Italian *Vogue*. She wants a bunch of English and Irish newspapers. She wants a copy of a new unauthorized biography about her. And most interestingly, she wants *Scandal Annual* 1991, a less than weighty tome that promises a guide to "Who got caught doing what in 1990." Flipping past the book's cover—which features a photo of her least favorite comedian, Andrew Dice Clay—O'Connor locates a section in the table of contents called "Boy, Is That Dumb!" that gathers "the year's most stupid actions and statements." She smiles and says quietly, "Well, I must be in there *somewhere*."

As it turns out, O'Connor is nowhere to be found in the *Scandal Annual*, but her fear is understandable. Since "Nothing Compares 2 U" hit Number One and made her a star a year ago, O'Connor has been in the news constantly—and usually for reasons unrelated to the brilliance of her music. In her year of living dangerously at the top, O'Connor has taken on all comers.

She and Frank Sinatra engaged in a surreal pissing match over her refusal to have the national anthem played

before one of her concerts. She and the Diceman clashed
when she canceled an appearance on *Saturday Night Live* because he was the host. Then O'Connor went public with
accusations that Prince—who wrote "Nothing Compares 2
U"—physically threatened her. Most recently, self-designated
fashion czar Mr. Blackwell placed her high on his list of the
worst-dressed women, calling her "the bald-headed banshee
of MTV" and "a new age nightmare."

"It's not like I got up in the morning and said, 'Okay,
now let's start a new controversy,'" O'Connor says. "I don't
do anything in order to cause trouble. It just so happens that
what I do naturally causes trouble. And that's fine with me.
I'm *proud* to be a troublemaker."

Of course, she has better reasons to be proud. All the recent commotion has at times threatened to obscure her real
achievement in the past year: namely, that with *I Do Not Want
What I Haven't Got*—a demanding, highly personal master-
piece—she proved that a recording artist could refuse to com-
promise and still connect with millions of listeners hungry for
music of substance. For this accomplishment, many honors
have come O'Connor's way—three MTV video awards, four
Grammy nominations, and now a virtual sweep of the *Rolling
Stone* Readers and Critics Polls. Readers voted O'Connor the
Artist of the Year and also named her tops in the Best Album
and Best Female Singer categories. (And, perhaps because she is
so controversial, she was also selected as Worst Female Singer by
the readers.) Critics were also at a loss for someone to compare
to O'Connor, giving her top honors in the Artist of the Year,
Best Album, Best Single, and Best Female Singer categories.

Over lunch at The Source—the famed LA health-food restaurant where Woody Allen and Diane Keaton face off at the end of *Annie Hall*—O'Connor, twenty-four, ignores such offerings as the Aware salad and the brown-rice pancakes, settling instead for eggs, cappuccino, and a steady stream of cigarettes. As she reviews the events of the past year, O'Connor occasionally switches the topic to something else she wants that she hasn't got—a man. "I'm *completely* in love with Andy Garcia," she says excitedly at one point. "I think it's a fucking tragedy that both he and Kevin Costner are married." A friend of hers expresses some disappointment with the appearance of Costner's butt in *Dances with Wolves*, but O'Connor declines to offer an opinion. "I couldn't say," she opines, "it's been so long since I've *seen* one." But her mood improves as she delivers some new information: that the guy she loves in the latest Janet Jackson video is both straight and single.

True to her reputation, O'Connor is no diplomat. Asked to list her favorite records of 1990, she offers an additional list of her least favorite. Yet, for all her well-chronicled feistiness, O'Connor is not the hairless hell-raiser so many stories would lead one to believe. In person there's a sweetness and generosity about her that doesn't translate to the tabloids. It's evident in the way she speaks with fans who approach her and in the way she quietly slips a twenty-dollar bill to a middle-aged homeless man on the street. Finally, though, it is not Sinéad O'Connor's personality that makes her Artist of the Year but the bravery and power of her remarkable music.

DAVID WILD: You've said that disruption and disturbance are not necessarily bad things. But do you think all the controversy of the last year has hurt you in any way?

SINÉAD O'CONNOR: No, I don't think it's hurt me at all. Otherwise, we wouldn't be doing this interview for the Readers and Critics Poll, *would* we? I don't look at all the things that happened as being disruptions or disturbances. I look at them as being incidents where I expressed how I felt about something, about what I saw to be the truth. And sometimes a lot of people didn't agree with me—which is to be expected.

WILD: You don't think it's had a bad effect on your public image?

O'CONNOR: I think that people aren't nearly as stupid as the media thinks they are. I don't think the media has *any* idea what people think. I find all the controversy funny now. The national anthem episode is the funniest thing that happened to me in my whole life. But at the time, I was *shitting* myself. I thought if the *New York Post* said, "Sinéad O'Connor snubs America," somebody would shoot me. I went to a Janet Jackson show, and she had these pyrotechnics. I fucking nearly *died* when they went off. I leapt out of my skin.

WILD: What turned you around?

O'CONNOR: It happened when I went outside in disguise at one of the shows where there was supposedly an enormous protest being launched. I felt much better because I could hear what the actual people in the crowd were saying. And they were saying the whole controversy was rubbish. I stopped being frightened, because I realized that the people who I was actually in any way concerned about were on my side. And that the media was just making a big deal because it sold newspapers.

WILD: Besides the time you went undercover, have you had many other chances to meet your fans?

O'CONNOR: Yes, but it's very different when they know who I am. Most of the time it's awkward, because they don't necessarily act like themselves.

WILD: Because of the nature of your work, it's obvious that your fans feel a deep connection with you. What sort of things do they say to you in fan mail?

O'CONNOR: I don't know. I don't read it.

WILD: Why not?

O'CONNOR: I'm very frightened of getting ideas about myself. It's not that I don't care about people, because I do. It takes a lot for somebody to actually write a letter to you, but I can't just sit there all day reading letters from people telling me I'm brilliant, because I'll fucking go *mad*. I might turn into the biggest *wanker* that ever walked the Earth, which I'm probably heading toward anyway at this stage.

WILD: The national anthem episode got much stranger when Sinatra put his two cents in.

O'CONNOR: That also scared the shit out of me at the very beginning because it was, you know, *Frank Sinatra*. But soon enough he turned his attention to George Michael.

WILD: Frank was turning into a rock critic for a while there.

O'CONNOR: Yeah. I mean, he was on some kind of roll. And obviously the man has a problem with women—*obviously* he has. But I don't have any problem with him.

WILD: Are you a fan of his music?

O'CONNOR: Yeah, I *love* Frank Sinatra. I've bought practically every fucking box set that his record companies have thrown out. I think he's brilliant.

WILD: Would you sing with him?

O'CONNOR: Oh, I don't know. I think it's more of a case of whether he would sing with *me*. Somehow I don't see it happening.

WILD: Fill in the blank: 1990 was the most _____ year of your life.

O'CONNOR: Jesus, it was just the *most*. It was the most intensely emotional year of my life. Every single emotion that a human being could possibly experience, I've experienced constantly and *intensely*. It was very traumatic. There were very good things about it. But it's been very, very disturbing, and I'm quite fucked up in a lot of ways at the moment as a consequence.

WILD: What was the high point of the year for you?

O'CONNOR: When I passed my driver's test. I finally have a license! Also, going to Ireland to do an awards ceremony. I've always felt quite condescended to by the Irish music business, and so I was quite pleased to be able to stand there and say I'm able to do something.

WILD: Why do you think they couldn't deal with you?

O'CONNOR: Because I was a woman doing something differ- ent. The kind of music I'm doing, it's not what Irish women are expected to do. At the beginning they didn't really see that there was anything to it. And so they were quite patron- izing about it.

WILD: How do you feel about the suggestion that you can only write when you're unhappy?

O'CONNOR: Well, they're not unhappy songs. What have I written that's unhappy? Name me an unhappy song.

WILD: "The Last Day of Our Acquaintance."

O'CONNOR: Yeah, but you see, for me that song isn't . . . it's not *unhappy*. It *resolves* itself. It's going through all of the feelings that you feel about a situation and ending on quite a fucking strong note. You know, I think the songs are quite optimistic.

WILD: Is there any song you've written that you'd describe as light?

O'CONNOR: I'd say "Jump in the River" is about the lightest song I've done.

WILD: And that's not exactly "Louie Louie."

O'CONNOR: No, I don't really like *light*. I'm not really a *light* person. I mean, there's so many other people doing *light*.

WILD: When you dominated the MTV Awards this year, people seemed surprised to see you up there smiling and enjoying yourself. It was as if your image was such that people didn't expect you to actually have fun.

O'CONNOR: People expect me to have a certain attitude toward awards ceremonies. They don't expect to see me freaking out over the fact that I've won an award, because I always said that I don't really give a shit about things like that. And I don't, professionally. But just as a human being, like as a young girl from Dublin, there I was in Los Angeles making acceptance speeches and having a blast. It was *fun*.

I'm more excited about the *Rolling Stone* Readers [and

Critics] Poll vote than I am about something like the Grammys, because it's a matter of actual people saying they like me. That's much more exciting, more real, than the Grammys, which are very political. This is not because you sold a lot of records or any kind of shit like that.

WILD: Your music is so much more complex and demanding than the standard stuff heard on the radio these days. Do you think your success is a fluke or part of a bigger trend?

O'CONNOR: People don't want to hear what's on the fucking radio. People are screaming out for something more. Look at the way records get to Number One in this country. It has to do with what people buy, but the other half has to do with what the fucking radio stations play. That's ridiculous. That's not an honest representation of what people like. How can it be?

WILD: Why do you think you were the one to break through?

O'CONNOR: I'm not the only one. It just so happens that I had a Number One record. But I'm not the only one. What about Van Morrison? Van Morrison ought to be fucking *canonized* as far as I'm concerned. *He* ought to win every Grammy for every category of every fucking award that there possibly is. Why doesn't he?

The media in this country doesn't encourage people to think. Turn on the radio or the TV—you don't see anything that inspires you or makes you think about anything. And that's the way people like to keep it. They don't want people to think for themselves. The only way that people are getting the opportunity to think for themselves at this moment is through music. And in particular, the hip-hop movement, which is why the censors are doing their fucking level best to stop it. It's complete racism. I would have been censored if it wasn't. Loads of people would be. Madonna would be. Madonna's records got to Number One. *Vanilla Ice*—let me make this point, "Ice Ice Baby" is a complete rip-off lyrically of N.W.A and loads of people. "Police are on the scene / You know what I mean"—as if Vanilla Ice ever had an experience with a policeman. If that can get to Number One, that makes me very suspicious. It's okay for Vanilla Ice—who is very all-American and white—to make violent records and talk about things like that. But it's not all right for N.W.A. N.W.A has had the same record out, except much better. It didn't get to Number One.

WILD: Some people accused you of censorship when you dropped out of *Saturday Night Live* to protest Andrew Dice Clay's appearance. Recently you said you've reconsidered your decision.

O'CONNOR: I wouldn't change what I did, because I had to do it in order to get to this realization. But I'm very opposed to the whole censorship thing. And so if I speak out against censorship and how I think that people should be exposed to N.W.A or Ice Cube if they want to be, then I have to allow for Andrew Dice Clay. Of course, I still don't like the guy. I think he's a *wanker*, I really do. And it's not just because of the feminist thing. It's because I have a huge problem with homophobia as well, and that's the worst thing that I think he does. But at the same time, I can't try and stop him.

WILD: Did you see that *Saturday Night Live?*

O'CONNOR: Yeah, I did. I mean, the whole show was based on the fact that myself and the other lady [Nora Dunn] had pulled out. So I wonder what it would have been about if we hadn't. But actually I was glad, because I had been madly in love with a bloke and the only time I could ever go out with him was that night. So it was all very convenient for me.

WILD: In recent interviews you seem to have given up on men.

O'CONNOR: Well, men are all the same, aren't they?

WILD: I don't know. Are they?

O'CONNOR: I think so.

WILD: How so?

O'CONNOR: Oh, they're all full of shit. They have no *balls.* Men have *no* balls.

WILD: And there are no exceptions to this rule?

O'CONNOR: I haven't met an exception to it, no. I haven't ever met a male that would be as prepared to live by himself, to be as true to himself, as a woman would be. You know, I've never met a man that had the balls to stick his neck out. Obviously, people do—people like Ice Cube or Ice-T—that's why I like people like that. But romantically I've never met a man like that. They allow themselves to be intimidated easily, and they can't express themselves. *Ugh*. Men are just a pain in the ass, they really are. But *of course* I would like Lancelot to come along and sweep me off to his castle. You know, I'm getting on a bit.

WILD: Let's talk hair. Have you ever considered letting it grow long so people would stop making a big deal about it?

O'CONNOR: No. The only time I've ever thought I should grow my hair is in order to get some man to fall madly in love with me. Men find me intimidating anyway and maybe even more intimidating because I have no hair. I don't really know why it's such a big deal to people. I suppose it's because it's not like anybody else's. It has certain associations as well. It has the whole fascist association. It has the whole lesbian association. And it has the whole aggressive-woman association, which, of course, everybody hates. Years ago, Chris Hill and Nigel Grainge [the heads of Ensign Records, O'Connor's label] wanted me to wear high-heel boots and tight jeans and grow my hair. And I decided that they were so pathetic that I shaved my head so there couldn't be any further discussion. I also did it for other reasons, but that told them. They wanted me to look like one of their wives, or one of their mistresses. I mean, can you imagine me in a pair of skintight black jeans and a pair of high-heel boots? I'd look ridiculous. I mean, if I thought I looked good in those things, I'd wear them.

WILD: Are you aware of people trying to look like you?

O'CONNOR: I've seen people with shaved heads, but I wouldn't flatter myself by assuming it was because of me.

WILD: So you don't feel you might be a role model?

O'CONNOR: I don't think I am.

WILD: How about a sex symbol?

O'CONNOR: Well, no. I've always wanted to be a sex symbol, but I don't think I am. I *hope* I am. Well, I can't imagine myself being one. I mean, I think I'm really hideous and ugly and fluffy and wrinkly and disgusting, so I can't imagine anyone thinking that I was sexually attractive. And if they do, where the fuck *are* they?

WILD: But hundreds of male writers have written endlessly about how beautiful your eyes are.

O'CONNOR: Yeah, but it's only my *eyes*. It is not anything else.

WILD: What are your impressions of life as a celebrity?

O'CONNOR: Basically, what I've encountered is a load of bullshit. Especially since being in Los Angeles. It amazes me how full of shit people are. It amazes me how into being famous a lot of people are and how they're so into it that they will introduce themselves to you by their band name rather than their own name or by whose wife they are. I wish that people could realize that people like me are just like them. I wish that they could realize that as much we do anything for them, they are doing it for us a hundredfold. Whatever healing that takes place through music is equally given back to the person that writes it. So we're all in it to help each other.

WILD: Have the experiences of the last year made you more or less spiritual?

O'CONNOR: More so. Much more so. I think that's because before any of this happened, I had a sufficient amount of training to be able to deal with everything from a philosophical point of view. Otherwise I'd probably be on smack. I'd probably be an alcoholic. I'd probably be dead if I wasn't able to see it from above and say, "Well, what can I learn from this?" Or, "What must I change about myself?"

WILD: Why did you decide to settle in Los Angeles?

O'CONNOR: I don't really know yet. At the moment I think the only reason I'm here is because I want to learn things, and my life has changed so much since I left England last year that I couldn't just go back to living in Golders Green. So I wanted to just have a new set of experiences.

WILD: Is there anything you miss about Ireland?

O'CONNOR: I miss the fact that people there are very honest. I don't see that here at all. I'm very, very frightened of this place and how full of shit everybody is. I miss the truth of the place. But Ireland has its own dishonesties as well.

WILD: What don't you miss?

O'CONNOR: I'm glad to be away from the things that I associate with my upbringing in Ireland, which wasn't happy at all. And so I'm glad to be away from things that remind me of that and away from the feeling of being trapped and the feeling of not being allowed to express myself and the feeling of being in some way an outcast because of being the kind of woman that I am.

WILD: In one recent magazine article, you discussed how you were abused by your mother. Have you ever regretted being so open with journalists about such personal topics?

O'CONNOR: No, the reason why I discussed that is because I believe very much that the reason why those things happen to people is because we are all brought up not to discuss them. The things that happened to me happened because of the society in which I lived, which was a society that did not—and still doesn't—express itself. And I think it's very dangerous to keep those kinds of things in.

WILD: You've also talked openly about some unpleasant experiences with Prince. I understand that you no longer want to sing "Nothing Compares 2 U" because of what happened.

O'CONNOR: Yeah. It spoiled the song completely for me. I feel a connection with the song, but the experience was a very disturbing one. At the moment, I really don't like the idea of singing the song. I need to get to the stage where I can separate the writer from the song—which I suppose I always did before. But I'm just very angry with him. Anyway, it's not like I'm going to spend the rest of my life singing the song that I had that went to Number One. That's not what I'm all about. I do other stuff, too. I mean, I've sung the song so many times that I'm bored with the song at this stage.

WILD: In concert, you struck me as being anything but bored. I've never seen a performer who seemed so emotionally committed to their performance.

O'CONNOR: This past year the concerts were like going through therapy because there was so much shit going on, on the road. Luckily, every night I had a show to do; otherwise I would have gone mental. There was an awful lot of very, very serious, traumatic stuff going on. It was just as well that I was on the road. But then as a result of being on the road, all these other traumatic things happened.

WILD: Was it especially hard being separated from your son while touring?

O'CONNOR: Yes. Very much so, very much so.

WILD: Does he have any idea what his mom does for a living?

O'CONNOR: Uh-uh. I just say that I sing songs.

WILD: What's the best Sinéad rumor you heard this year?

O'CONNOR: I think that I'm having Lenny Kravitz's baby. I mean, I wouldn't mind. And Peter Gabriel's baby, too.

WILD: Is it a boy or a girl?

O'CONNOR: I don't know yet. I haven't read the papers. One of the funniest things, actually, was recently in one of those really tacky soap magazines. They had something about how I was a big fibber because I was a feminist yet I used to be a kissogram girl. And I fail to make the connection.

WILD: Is there any music you wouldn't want your son listening to—like, say, the Geto Boys?

O'CONNOR: I would want him to listen to whatever he wanted to listen to. I think people like the Geto Boys and N.W.A serve a very useful function. Apart from the fact that they are expressing what life is like for some people—and that's why some other people have a problem with it. If you believe that music is to express human feelings, then you've got to acknowledge that aggression is a human feeling as well, and that it is far better for somebody to go into their car and listen to "Fuck tha Police" than to actually go and blow up a policeman. You know, rap is the only type of music that I know that expresses all of the human feelings and encourages people to make something of themselves.

WILD: Earlier, you offered to give a list of the records you hated last year. Which ones were they?

O'CONNOR: Oh, dear, can I do this? Why not? Fuck it, it could be a *very* long list. I hate MC Hammer's record. I hate Vanilla Ice's record with a vengeance. I hate Whitney Houston's record, that "I'm Your Baby Tonight." I *hate* that. What else? There's an AC/DC record out.

WILD: "Moneytalks"?

O'CONNOR: No.

WILD: "Thunderstruck"?

O'CONNOR: Oh, God, his voice is just *horrendous*, it really is.

WILD: What do you think of another MTV staple, Guns n' Roses?

O'CONNOR: I saw an interview with Axl Rose on the television, and I thought he was really really lovely, I really did. My friend Ciara and I were talking about him yesterday, about how you just want to bring him home and give him a bowl of soup. He's like a little kid, *isn't* he? He just seemed that he really needed some mothering or something. We want to tell Slash we love him as well. And Mike Tyson.

WILD: You've said that while you were growing up your big influences were Bob Dylan and Barbra Streisand.

O'CONNOR: They were, but I'd say that at the moment my biggest influences are hip-hop people. Not musically, but personally. My biggest influences are people like Ice Cube. Ice-T is an enormous influence. I saw his concert and nearly wet myself. Also Public Enemy, Van Morrison, and another Irishman called Christy Moore. Also Roseanne Barr.

WILD: Roseanne Barr?

O'CONNOR: She's amazing. I saw her on TV the other day, when she went on about Arsenio Hall. I just thought that she was the most incredible woman I've ever seen.

WILD: Considering recent events, perhaps the two of you could collaborate on a rap version of the national anthem.

O'CONNOR: I wouldn't sing the national anthem.

WILD: Don't like the tune?

O'CONNOR: I think of the lyrics of the song as being very dangerous. I think if you are into censorship, you should censor that, frankly. "Bombs bursting in air" and the "rockets' red glare" isn't anything that I'm interested in singing about. And yet N.W.A piss everyone off singing about AK-47s.

WILD: Do you have goals for this year?

O'CONNOR: No. What I'd like to happen is to return to normal.

WILD: Do you think that's possible?

O'CONNOR: Yeah, I do. I think it has to happen. I just need to forget that I'm *Sinéad O'Connor*, you know. I need to be whoever I was a year ago, before all this happened.

WILD: As the song says, do you feel so different now?

O'CONNOR: Oh, yeah. I feel even *more* different now. Absolutely.

SPECIAL CHILD

INTERVIEW BY BOB GUCCIONE, JR.
SPIN
NOVEMBER 1991

Days before the Grammy Awards last February, in the dark heart of the bombing of Baghdad, Sinéad O'Connor dropped a couple of her own bombshells: she was boycotting the Grammys in protest of the Gulf War and quitting the music business. The preposterous notion that anyone would particularly care is exactly what gave these pronouncements their weight. Sinéad's conviction that these were significant responses to the war and the music industry's apathy made them so. They were reported—and discussed—worldwide.

Record sales alone don't make Sinéad that important: the raw, unmeditated genuineness of her rebellion does. She's a spokesperson because she speaks. In today's homogeneous, timid American society, that's all it takes.

The previous August, Sinéad had caused a tremendous stir by refusing to allow an arena to play the national anthem before her concert. The press rose like a mob to lynch her. Through the furor she protested she'd been misunderstood and issued a carefully constructed press release trying to explain her position. In reality, no explanation would have mattered to the war-frenzied mob. America was finally going to give itself amnesty for Vietnam, and no head-shaved, Irish, twenty-three-year-old woman was going to interfere with that.

Unapologetic, Sinéad withdrew to London, where she lives, and studied acting. She says she's going to play Joan of Arc in the planned movie. In July 1991 she released *My Special Child*, a four-song EP, donating the revenues to the International Red Cross Kurdish Relief program.

We met at her manager's West London office and talked in an insufferably hot conference room with the windows shut to keep the midday noise out. She thought it was going to be a three-cigarette interview, laying them out neatly, side by side, in front of her like pencils. It turned out to be a nine-cigarette interview.

When it was over, I played with her four-year-old son Jake while she went to make some phone calls. He kept kicking me—his idea of fun. I picked him up and held him by his ankles, upside down over my shoulder—my idea of fun. "You smell pooey," he announced shrilly.

"You've got a lot of balls for someone upside down in mid-air," I told him. Then I realized: that describes Sinéad perfectly.

SPIN: What made you want to do the *My Special Child* record?

SINÉAD O'CONNOR: I had written the song from my own experience. I wanted to put it out and use the money to raise awareness of child abuse. Then the Kurdish thing came up and seemed really urgent, so thought I'd do that. The song itself is about my experience with having had an abortion last year and how I dealt with that and how it made me feel.

SPIN: What made you want to get an abortion?

O'CONNOR: Well, I didn't really want to. The pregnancy had been planned, and I was madly in love with the father of the child. However, things didn't really work out between us. We were fighting. I was on tour, and I was feeling sick all the time. I didn't know what to do, and he wasn't really interested in the child. So I was left with the decision of whether or not to have the child, knowing that the father wasn't going to be around. I decided that it was better not to and that I would have a child at a later stage when his father would be around and involved. I didn't feel that I could handle it by myself.

SPIN: Did that trouble you deeply?

O'CONNOR: Yeah, because it was planned and I was very happy about it. I'd had three miscarriages previously, and I was quite worried about whether I was going to be able to hold on to the pregnancy and it looked like I was going to. So I was very distraught; it wasn't a decision that I made lightly or that anyone makes lightly. It took me a year to get over it, but it was the right decision. I just believe that if a child is meant to be born it will be born. It doesn't really matter whether you have an abortion or a miscarriage. The whole issue is pro-choice. I wouldn't lobby for or against abortion, but I would lobby very strongly for the right of women to have control over their own bodies and make decisions for themselves. Nobody has the right to tell anyone else what to think or believe. Especially the Catholic Church with the amount of murdering and pillaging that it's done.

SPIN: How much influence has growing up Catholic had on you?

O'CONNOR: It was never a really large part of my life. I always believed in God and the Virgin Mary and the immaculate conception and I love those things. So I just took from Catholicism what I loved about it, which was the image of her and all those sorts of stories. But I didn't feel that it fucked me up at all; I didn't really take it that seriously. I just took from it what I liked and what made sense to me and what appealed to me. I would have had the beliefs that I have anyway.

SPIN: Do you believe in heaven and hell?

O'CONNOR: No, I don't believe in heaven or hell. I don't believe in any sort of burning. I don't believe it's right to teach children that God is somebody that will punish them if they misbehave, that God isn't somebody who understands. That's an abuse of children.

SPIN: Do you believe in heaven?

O'CONNOR: I believe in different levels of spiritual attainment and the highest level is something that somebody like Christ achieved. The highest level of spiritual attainment is the closest thing to heaven. But I don't believe in heaven and hell as they're depicted.

SPIN: You grew up in Ireland, surrounded by all this Catholic mythology.

O'CONNOR: I can sift off the bullshit because there's what's called the church triumphant and the church militant. The church triumphant is basically God and the saints and everybody else; the church militant is the church on Earth, which I have no respect for.

SPIN: When you were growing up you were surrounded by great pain. Did you think that God had deserted you?

O'CONNOR: No, I believed in God very much. I didn't believe there was anything to punish me [for] or I didn't believe I had been deserted. I always believed and prayed all the time and took great comfort particularly from the mother of God.

SPIN: Were you lonely as a child?

O'CONNOR: Yeah, I would say that I was, but I don't think I knew that I was lonely. But I found it very difficult to speak to people. I just sat at the back of the class like this [*hunches over*], and that's why my posture is so bad. I never spoke to anybody and I didn't socialize. I didn't know how to. I couldn't up to a year ago even look a person in the face when I was talking to them.

SPIN: Why were you so shy, and how did you overcome it a year ago?

O'CONNOR: I forced myself to get over it, and I'm not particularly over it. But I forced myself because I couldn't function and I just couldn't continue to be that way. What made me that way was the abuse and the subsequent lack of assistance or understanding from anybody outside my home situation.

SPIN: What age are you talking about here? Eight years old?

O'CONNOR: Smaller than that even. If a child is being abused it will react in any number of different ways. What I did was I went into myself. I couldn't communicate with anybody; I couldn't study. I could read and write but I had no interest in it; I couldn't get out of my own head.

SPIN: Were you physically terrified?

O'CONNOR: Yeah, I grew up in a state of terror, constantly. I'm one of millions of people who grew up in the same situation, who grew up terrified constantly.

SPIN: What did you think of? Did you fantasize about things that later became songs?

O'CONNOR: Yeah, I lived in a fantasyland; that's how I survived.

SPIN: I grew up in a broken marriage, which was, thank God, not abusive. The family was very together. But I was effectively running the family at fifteen.

O'CONNOR: Well, that's abuse.

SPIN: Yeah, but a mild form.

O'CONNOR: Well, what abuse constitutes is not allowing a child to be itself, not allowing a child to be a child.

SPIN: Don't you think the real world does that anyway?

O'CONNOR: It shouldn't.

SPIN: Well, in a perfect world it wouldn't.

O'CONNOR: It can be a perfect world. The cause of all of the world's problems, as far as I'm concerned, is child abuse. It's the lack of understanding of children and of what they are and of the fact that they must be allowed to be themselves and form their own opinions and make decisions for themselves. From the moment a child is born, certainly in America and I think everywhere else, but it's most obvious in America, the child is conditioned.

Everything that the child will see on the television or will learn in school or will hear on the radio or read in the magazines, or anything that it's exposed to, is set out to form this child into a specific kind of person, one who doesn't think for itself, one who doesn't have opinions of its own and one who has no spirit of its own. From the time a child sets foot in school, it's fucked, as far as being itself is concerned. You may not ask questions, you may not have opinions of your own. You just learn what you're taught in your history book, which is all lies, and that is what you must believe.

SPIN: Do you think that the media deprograms people?

O'CONNOR: I think it has been very cleverly employed to condition people. Certainly America is the most obvious example, although it's the same all over the world. I think that television should be abolished completely. I think it's completely destructive and there's nothing positive about it, nothing at all.

SPIN: What about MTV?

O'CONNOR: It should be abolished.

SPIN: Why do you say that?

O'CONNOR: Because TV has killed free thinking. TV has killed art, it's killed poetry, it's killed theater, it's killed all those kinds of things. It conditions people; they just sit in front of it all day and believe what it tells them. Apart from that, purely from a scientific point of view—MTV being the worst example of this—if an image keeps changing really quickly your brain doesn't learn to concentrate, and it gets so that you can't concentrate because you get so used to seeing things only for a second that you don't take in what you're seeing. It's not good for people who want to study or learn something.

We as a race have lost our spirituality. We've lost contact with who we are and what our purpose for existence is and we've lost contact with God. The reason for that is that we started going into other people's countries and wiping out races and wiping out cultures in order to achieve, materially.

Through the loss of our spirituality, we feel empty. We have an enormous hole in ourselves and I don't think that anyone can say that they don't feel a huge emptiness in their lives, which they try to fill materially, because that is all they see on television or in the paper. They see that people who achieve materially are happy, so to fill their emptiness that's what they go for. They go for drugs, they go for alcohol, they go for sex, they go for cigarettes, all to fill up the void. Never anywhere do they see any information telling them that they could fill it in another way. That if you have peace within yourselves, that you will attract peaceful things.

You're taught that you've got to go to work for a living. You've got to do a fucking job that you hate, just so that you can earn enough money to put food in your mouth and never will you discover who you are or what you can actually do.

The basic problem of the whole world is child abuse.

SPIN: That's an incredibly sweeping definition.

O'CONNOR: If you look throughout history, all serial killers have been abused as children. All of them, without exception. All alcoholics have been abused as children. All drug addicts. All rapists. All sexual offenders have been abused as children. Hitler was an abused child; Saddam Hussein was an abused child.

SPIN: How did you get over it? You've got great strength and courage.

O'CONNOR: Well, the word *courage* means quite literally being afraid but going on. I'm still getting over it, but how I got over it was realizing that the cause was that nobody said anything about it. It was a continuing cycle—it's a cycle of abuse. A child is abused, it never expresses itself because it's never encouraged to express itself. It's encouraged just to shut the fuck up. I realized there was an ongoing cycle. I realized that I was very, very fucked up and that I had to do a lot of work on myself and that I had to go and get help.

SPIN: Did you see a therapist?

O'CONNOR: No. What I believe in most are the 12-step groups—whether they're Alcoholics Anonymous or Narcotics Anonymous. There's one that's called Adult Children of Alcoholics/Dysfunctional Families, and that's where I went.

SPIN: And that helped?

O'CONNOR: Yeah, absolutely. It helps you to learn that it's not your fault how fucked up you are and everything else is not your fault. I keep thinking of the people that are in college in America, the people that would be around the same age as me, or younger, and I imagine that there are an awful lot of them who have experienced abuse of one kind or another. And I'm trying to explain it so that they will understand that you get to a stage where you just think you are a piece of shit—that's what it does to you; you think that you're a piece of shit. You think that you are worthless; you think you're ugly. Every time you look in the mirror you just see an ugly wanker.

SPIN: Do you feel that way?

O'CONNOR: Yeah, I do.

SPIN: You're incredibly beautiful.

O'CONNOR: I have no concept of that.

SPIN: But why not? I'm not the first guy that has said that.

O'CONNOR: It doesn't matter what anyone says. I stand on-stage maybe seven nights a week with five thousand people applauding me and telling me I'm wonderful, but it doesn't make any difference to me, because I don't love myself. Now I do, but up to that point I didn't. It doesn't matter who tells you you're wonderful if you don't think it and if your mother and father didn't think it. You're never going to think it unless you work on yourself and learn that you are lovable.

SPIN: What do you recommend to people who have been abused?

O'CONNOR: The first thing that I would say to those people is that I have felt exactly as I know those people feel. And you have to acknowledge, in the first place, that you have been affected and that you have every right to say, yes, you've been abused and you've been treated badly and unfairly. A lot of the time I felt if I talked about the abuse that I was making a big deal out of nothing, which of course is bullshit. You think that you've no right to the feelings you feel because that's what you've been told all your life. You've been beaten up for feeling the way you feel. So you start to build up a false self in order to please everybody, to make them like you.

I would say go to the 12-step groups or read the John Bradshaw/Alice Miller books. They are huge proponents of the adult-child syndrome, which is literally this—that if a child experiences something that's very, very shocking and traumatic it will cut itself off from experiencing the thing consciously. Their brain cuts out because it's too shocking for them so they only experience it subconsciously. They don't feel anything. It can be scared by it, but it doesn't know what it feels. And the feelings build up and build up and build up as you grow up. You are literally arrested at that stage of your development. You are three years of age walking around in a fifty-year-old body. The world is being run by adult children.

It's literally that you are living in here [*indicates her torso*] and you are this size [*holds her hands two feet apart*] and you are in a grown-up body. I used to have tantrums at twenty-one years of age; I used to behave like a three-year-old child. I had no idea what I was doing. I used to look at myself and say, "What the fuck are you doing?" even while I would be doing it. Screaming and being upset and not being able to get out of bed, you know, just crying all day long, just really fucking angry, and wanting to just be a bitch to people. And I would have no control over myself. You are being controlled by your child. It is literally the puppet master. And you need to get in touch with it and to help it grow up. It's terrified.

SPIN: What were your individual experiences?

O'CONNOR: I experienced abuse on every level that you can imagine. My mother was a very unhappy woman, who was very, very violent and found it very difficult to cope with life, because of obviously her own experiences as a child. I was beaten up very severely with every kind of implement you can imagine yourself being beaten with. And I was starved; I was locked in my room for days at a time without being fed, with no clothes. I was made to sleep in the garden of my house overnight. I lived for a summer in the garden of my house.

SPIN: How old were you?

O'CONNOR: At that stage, I was about twelve. But earlier than that I had been made to sleep with my brothers and my sister in the garden and I had been starved, et cetera. And I had been psychologically abused by being told that I was a piece of shit all my life, that it was my fault that my parents split up. That I was dirty, I was filthy, that I was kinky. I was, you know, basically a piece of shit because I was a girl and that I was never any good.

SPIN: Were you the oldest?

O'CONNOR: No, my brother was the oldest. I was beaten up every single day and so were the others. Very, very badly. I lived my life in a state of terror. Merely the sounds of my mother's feet on the hearth ceiling were enough to send us into spasms of complete terror. We were neglected, we were beaten, we were abused psychologically and emotionally.

SPIN: When did it stop?

O'CONNOR: When I left my mother, when I was thirteen. I want to point out that I have worked everything out with my family about this. And I love my mother and my father very much indeed. I'm not saying, "Bastards," or "Woe is me," or all that stuff, which is an important point for me to make for my family. But also for other people that it can be done.

I had always been encouraged to steal and one of the ways we made sure my mother didn't beat us up was to come home with money and things like that, so myself and my sister stole. We never went to bed before two o'clock in the morning, we never did homework, so I never did well in school. I have no qualifications at all as a result of it; we were always sick; we were always completely fucked up. So by the time I left, I didn't know who the fuck I was or what I was doing. I had always been in trouble with the police for stealing. So when I went to live with my father, suddenly I had all this freedom and I didn't know how to deal with it. So I started flunking out of school and still stealing. I got sent to this place called a rehabilitation center for girls with behavior problems. But at no stage was I rehabilitated or were any of the other girls. They were nice people, but nobody ever sat me down and worked with me in order to rehabilitate me back into society. And I was punished basically for being who I was again and rejected for being who I was again. For being what my parents had made me into, and what society had made my parents into.

It isn't enough to take a child from its family. The parents of the children need help. It's not enough to take their children from them or lock them up. The laws need to be changed as far as what can be done to help a child. The police used to come to our house on numerous occasions because the neighbors heard us screaming and they'd phone, and the police would come in and they'd just say, "Is everything all right?" and we'd be shitting ourselves because we couldn't say it wasn't all right 'cause what the fuck were they going to do about it? Go back again and then we'd get the shit kicked out of us if we said it wasn't all right, so we'd just sit there and say, "Yeah, everything is fine." And they'd go off again.

There's nothing that the police can do; there should be more help from government for women with children. Women lose themselves when they have children. Women shouldn't be told that they need to be in the home twenty-four hours a day, seven days a week because that's just not right. A woman needs to be herself and have her own life. So governments should help with things like that.

I grew up being told that I was ugly, that my body was something to be ashamed of, that sex was something to be ashamed of and that if you liked it, you were like a slut, a piece of shit. And I was not told that sex was something that naturally happened between two people who really loved and understood each other. I was taught by the media that sex was something I could just do with anybody and that it was perfectly acceptable. I was told that by rock 'n' roll as well.

SPIN: Was that appealing when rock 'n' roll told you that?

O'CONNOR: Sex seems to be the only situation in which people can feel love. It's the only place that they can feel intimacy so they go around doing it with everybody left, right, and center. And it doesn't work. It just doesn't work like that. That's what we see so that's what we go for. If we saw something else, we might go for that.

SPIN: Did the church confuse you about sex?

O'CONNOR: As far as I'm concerned, the church has no right to open up its mouth about sex for these reasons. First of all, none of them ever have sex, at least they're not supposed to. The second reason is that they do have sex. Priests in Ireland at the time of the abortion referendum were going around fucking young girls and getting them pregnant. I know of many instances. I know a woman who has been having an affair with a priest for the last twenty years. He has been a priest throughout the abortion referendum, the divorce referendum, et cetera. Now if she had become pregnant, what would he have done? I know of another case of a priest who got a girl pregnant and made her go to London and have an abortion and met her back off the boat, looking at his watch to make sure he could get back in time for mass. At the time of the abortion referendum. They can't fucking say a word about it, because they're all shagging left, right, and center, and they can sue me for that but it's the fucking truth. They should not open their mouths.

SPIN: What about the way sex is portrayed in rap?

O'CONNOR: Of course, there's sexism, but if you're going to give out about it in Black music, then give the fuck out about it in white music, too. There are examples of it all over the place of appalling videos of women being abused. What about that *Cherry Pie* record with the video with the girl being hosed down? I mean, what's that saying? What about "Love in an Elevator"? What's that all about? Teaching people that they can just go and pick up some girl in an elevator and have sex with her?

SPIN: It's all about fantasy, Black or white. Rock 'n' roll aims at being entertaining fantasy.

O'CONNOR: I don't believe that rock 'n' roll is all about entertainment.

SPIN: I don't either, but it's certainly an entertainment medium.

O'CONNOR: It has become purely an entertainment medium.

SPIN: It was always going to.

O'CONNOR: No, no it wasn't. Look at the sixties. Yeah, there were always entertainers and other people—communicators—and everyone got their records played. And then people began to realize that these people had far too much power and they stopped playing the records of the communicators. The entertainers are the ones that are pushed to the forefront, the ones that don't really say anything about anything but they just write really nice songs that everyone enjoys, which are great, but the rest of us get pushed back. We don't get our

records played; we don't win Grammys. We don't win awards
for our ability to . . .

SPIN: You get your records played.

O'CONNOR: I don't. "Nothing Compares 2 U" got played. I
never got a record played before that and I probably won't get
one played since.

SPIN: I think you will.

O'CONNOR: I don't think so. It's nothing to do with the audience. Because the audience only know what they hear and if
they don't hear everything then obviously they can't form an
opinion.

SPIN: Isn't this a chicken-or-the-egg thing, though? I mean
the radio playlist and the MTV heavy-rotation list comes
down to what the audience requests.

O'CONNOR: They request what they're used to.

SPIN: Do you think England and America have become apa-
thetic, sleepy societies?

O'CONNOR: We've been made sleepy. We've been made to not
want anything, into a race that questions nothing. There is no
concept of the evil that goes on, of the manipulation and the
controlling. That everything they see has been fed to them
in order to make them into a kind of person who will not

question everything, who will fight for America, and think that they're doing a fucking good thing.

SPIN: What did you think about the Gulf War?

O'CONNOR: I thought that it was despicable. I thought it was despicable because people were lied to and the truth will come out about that war.

SPIN: I thought it was disgusting because it wasn't liberation we were reveling in, which was the one positive thing that came out of it.

O'CONNOR: That's not why the war happened. Do you think America gave a shit about the people in Kuwait? What about what happened in Panama?

SPIN: Stay on Kuwait. The U.S. essentially encouraged Iraq to invade Kuwait, we know that for a fact, but what I'm getting at is that there wasn't a celebration of the fact that brother mankind was liberated. It was a celebration that we beat the shit out of somebody.

O'CONNOR: That's what we've been made into. We're quite willing for our own sons to be killed for that reason. We think that that's a good thing. We don't question. We don't say, "Well, why is my son in Kuwait?" We say, "My son's in Kuwait, isn't it great?" That's abuse of children. The fact that they're selling to young children Gulf War stickers for their albums is disgusting. Completely disgusting. If all of the money they used on weapons was used for something constructive, was fed back into the earth, there is no reason in this day and age why every single person on this planet shouldn't have enough to eat. Every day in this world forty thousand children are starving to death, starving. Picture the image of your child starving to death. That's happening to forty thousand women today. There is no need for that.

SPIN: When you refused to let the national anthem be played before your concert, very few people defended your position.

O'CONNOR: And nobody defended me during the Grammy thing, which I will remember. Nobody. When the whole thing happened at the beginning of this year. No fucker defended me, they're all chickenshit. I'm talking about artists.

SPIN: I thought it was interesting that people, like FM DJs, who are normally the most left-wing liberals, who play records like "Ohio" on the anniversary of Kent State, and "Give Peace a Chance," wanted to hang you.

O'CONNOR: That's trendy though. South Africa is trendy, Neil Young is trendy. It's safe.

SPIN: Why do you think people wanted to kick you out of the country?

O'CONNOR: Because I'm a girl, for a start. They would not be nearly as offended by it if I was a man. A woman with a shaved head who wears Doc Martens, who doesn't comply with what is expected of women, who hasn't come through school and grown up to be what they wanted her to be, complaining about the American national anthem. They want to tell everyone that I'm civil.

SPIN: Looking back on the incident, would you do it differently?

O'CONNOR: No, absolutely not. I'm proud of it. Until my dying day I will be proud of that and of the Grammy thing. You know, put your fucking seatbelts on 'cause I haven't finished yet.

SPIN: It's rare today, Sinéad, to encounter that kind of stand taking.

O'CONNOR: We have no spirituality, that's what's wrong. We have no sense of what the fuck we're here for. We have no sense of—Jesus came here to show us that the truth was worth dying for. Jesus chose to be crucified, a most agonizing death and he shat himself. Don't let anybody say that he wasn't afraid. He sweated blood. But he did that rather than say that what he was saying wasn't the truth. And I believe that, and that's what I took from religion was that Jesus came to show me that the truth was worth fucking dying for.

SPIN: What happens if your next record comes out and your record company says, "Sinéad, you've got to apologize for this anthem thing 'cause no one's going to play it."

O'CONNOR: I don't give a shit whether I never get played on the radio or not, 'cause I just do what I do for myself and my record company understands that. They'd be cutting off their noses to spite their faces—do you think they're going to say that, for Christ's sake, you know? And anyway, they're not stupid. They know that I'm not one in a million. I'm merely expressing the feelings of millions of people. I just have a platform to air those views, and I'm operating for loads of people. I'm operating for all the abused children and all the women and all of the people who have been completely and utterly oppressed.

SPIN: Is there really a societal fear of women?

O'CONNOR: Yes, and that's why women have been controlled. The women who are admired are the ones that have blond hair and big lips and wear red lipstick and wear short skirts, because that's an acceptable image of a woman.

SPIN: Why?

O'CONNOR: Because it's safe. It's not threatening; it's not intimidating. I'm threatening and I'm intimidating because I don't conform to any of those things and I just say what I think. Madonna is probably the hugest model for women in America. There's a woman who people look up to as being a woman who campaigns for women's rights. A woman who, in an abusive way toward me, said that I looked [like] I had a run-in with a lawnmower and that I was about as sexy as a venetian blind. Now there's the woman that America looks up to as being a campaigner for women, slagging off another woman for not being sexy.

SPIN: What's the answer for women? I mean, I don't think you want to take that radical feminist . . .

O'CONNOR: No, I'm not a feminist or an anything-ist. I'm just a humanist. I believe in human beings, and believe in God. And I live my life through the things that I believe. That's all. I have a sense of why I'm on the earth, of where I go afterward.

SPIN: What drives you? What motivates you?

O'CONNOR: My belief in God motivates me.

SPIN: Do you see Jake as a manifestation of God?

O'CONNOR: Yeah, I do.

SPIN: When I first met you at *SPIN* one day, you struck me as very shy. Today you are certainly not shy. Do you feel that you turn the adversity in your life into fuel?

O'CONNOR: I don't let the adversity stop me, and I know the truth; I've seen examples of the existence of the truth and the existence of God. The examples are everywhere. I know that the truth is worth fighting for and worth dying for. It's worth anything. It's like Keith Richards said about his problem with the authorities and drugs: "I don't live by your petty rules."

And I don't have to. And if there is anything I want to do, it is to show to everybody else that they don't have to either.

SPIN: Do you think that you are a moral person?

O'CONNOR: Yeah, I am extremely moral.

SPIN: Do you think you are a good person?

O'CONNOR: Yeah, I'm trying to be good. I'm not a bad person. I do my best to be as good as I can be. Or, rather, I do my best to live by the word of God.

I think organized religion is a crutch. 'Cause it's controlling. Organized religion tells you what to think, what to believe, tells you who to be. I don't believe in one Catholic Church. I believe in every church. I believe in Buddhism. I believe in Hinduism. I believe in every religion. I believe you can take things from every religion. There is only one God. It's just different interpretations and many different things to learn. You shouldn't shut one out.

I used to lie in bed terrified at night thinking that I was going to burn in hell. It's an abuse to tell a child that God sees everything and knows what you think about and that you are going to be burned in hell. It's a huge abuse to teach children that God is not within themselves. That God is pollution. That God is bigger than them. That God is outside them. That is a lie. That's what causes the emptiness of children.

SPIN: Which artists do you think give a damn about anything other than their own success?

O'CONNOR: I think that the hip-hop movement cares. It has its negative aspects—

SPIN: N.W.A couldn't give a damn.

O'CONNOR: N.W.A are relevant because they are speaking a truth. They are speaking about what life is like for some people. And if you don't like what N.W.A are saying then you've got to find out why they are saying it. What makes young men grow up with those attitudes toward women? Child abuse.

SPIN: What about Public Enemy?

O'CONNOR: I think Public Enemy have done a hell [of an] amount of good. I think Professor Griff is a fucking madman. I think he is completely mental. But otherwise I think they've done a hell of a lot of good. The hip-hop movement, as far as I'm concerned, and the reggae movement have done so much good, more than I have ever experienced.

SPIN: It's fascinating to hear you say that because rap takes such a beating because of the sexism elements.

O'CONNOR: Why doesn't heavy metal?

SPIN: Because it's predominantly white, I guess.

O'CONNOR: Exactly. It's all right for white men to be sexy. It's not all right for Black men to be sexy. The second we as white women started to become attracted to Black men, that's when the trouble started. The second we started thinking, "Oh, these are nice people," that's when the trouble started. They don't want us having Black men's babies. They don't want us understanding the Black man and the Black race.

SPIN: Everyone has to be careful not to buy their own bullshit? How do you achieve that?

O'CONNOR: I question myself constantly. And because of my spiritual beliefs, I think it helps a lot of the time not to have a huge opinion of yourself. But because God knows if I'm being a fucking wanker.

SPIN: How do you handle celebrity?

O'CONNOR: You get used to it. I didn't like it at all and there are aspects of it that I don't like, but that's what I've been given.

SPIN: Do you find that celebrity insulates you from the world?

O'CONNOR: You mean makes it so that I don't necessarily know what life is like for other people?

SPIN: I mean that you're not treated the same way as the average person is.

O'CONNOR: But I am an average person, and I am treated in the same way. I experience a lot of prejudice because of my look, because of who I am, what I am, and what I stand for. The same as everybody else.

SPIN: It's because you intimidate people.

O'CONNOR: Not on purpose. They are intimidated by me because I don't conform to what they expect because I have a shaved head, because I'm outspoken and direct. But if they are intimidated by that, it's not my problem. I have to struggle with that, but I mustn't lose myself in the struggle. I think one thing celebrity does, it's provided me with a platform upon which and through which I can actually make a difference, to some extent. And that is what I intend to do.

SPIN: Do you feel alone?

O'CONNOR: No, no, I don't. I did feel very isolated, yeah. Because people have preconceived ideas about you and what kind of person you are.

SPIN: Are you working on any new music now?

O'CONNOR: No.

SPIN: Do you intend to in the near future?

O'CONNOR: Not for a long time, no.

SPIN: How long? A year?

O'CONNOR: I have no idea, but I have nothing left to say musically at the moment.

SPIN: I think, to a degree, people like your controversialness.

O'CONNOR: Far more than the media made it out to be. 'Cause I never received an offensive letter from anybody. I've received hundreds and hundreds of letters of support from real people.

SPIN: How do you galvanize other artists to take as forceful a stand as you do?

O'CONNOR: You don't. You just galvanize yourself. I gave up with other artists.

SPIN: You tried?

O'CONNOR: I expected other people to put their money where their mouths have been during the Grammys controversy. But now I give up. I'm just gonna do myself what I want to do, and they can all go and fuck themselves. Either they are with me or not; I don't care. I think that if you look at the hip-hop movement, they are the only people that have fought for the truth in any way, and they are the ones who are probably the most browbeaten. It is easy to browbeat them because they are Black.

SPIN: They are also intimidating and threatening.

O'CONNOR: Because they are Black. Because you know that when you are in a room full of Black people that they might have a right to have a problem with you.

SPIN: Who are your heroes today?

O'CONNOR: The Black people are my heroes. Bob Marley is a huge hero of mine. I think that the African culture and the people who have fought for the survival of the African culture are my heroes and my role models. The Buddhists are my role models.

SPIN: Do you love easily? Is it easy for you to fall in love?

O'CONNOR: Oh yeah. It's not easy for me to show love. It's not easy for me to feel comfortable with the expression of either verbal or physical love because I'm—of course, I don't know, self-conscious or I'm not so sure of myself.

SPIN: In child abuse, what part of it is, in your mind, unintended?

O'CONNOR: It's all unintended.

SPIN: It's all unintended?

O'CONNOR: It's just adult children with their children. All of it was unintended.

SPIN: Did you ever talk to your mother about this?

O'CONNOR: No, my mother died long before I could talk to her about it, but I know that she knows what I think and how I feel. But I've spoken to my father a good bit about it. It's all unintended.

SPIN: Was he aware of it going on?

O'CONNOR: Yeah, he was. And he did his level best; he did everything he could do, that he had the capacity to do. It's all unintended.

SPIN: Did you in your heart of hearts wish he would have just come by with a van one night and taken you kids away?

O'CONNOR: Well, he did that, he did that. But we wanted our mother, too.

SPIN: You would rather go back?

O'CONNOR: Yeah, the thing is, instead of the children going to one parent or another parent, the parent needs help. You know, none of it is intended; that is the terrible, terrible sadness of it all. It's just wasted lives, you know?

SPIN: Do you wish now you could talk to your mother? Do you wish she was sitting here right now?

O'CONNOR: No, because she and all the rest of us are better off with her being dead, to tell you the truth. I have a better relationship with her now that she is dead than I ever had with her when she was alive. I remember talking to her about it before she died and I said, "Why did you hit us? Why did you do that?" And she said, "I never did anything to you." You know, she believed that she hadn't done anything, because it was too shocking for her to deal with. Now, I know for a fact that she used to be really upset after she had done it because my father told me that she'd be devastated. I think that she had—and this is what my father thinks she had—this sort of predisposition to be unhappy. She had all the circumstances in her life by which she could have been happy. Like me. And she just couldn't be happy. She couldn't express herself; she couldn't give love. You know, she must have experienced some kind of abuse when she was a child. She couldn't express love at all. She just couldn't cope. I love my mother. I've always loved my mother. I always understood that she didn't mean to do what she did. I never hated her; I never had any grudge against her. I always understood that she was in a lot of pain and didn't know what she was doing.

SPIN: Do you find your celebrity is a problem in your family?

O'CONNOR: Absolutely. It's been a huge, huge source of awfulness. Because our family was so fucked up anyway that it was easy to blame the fucked-upness on me and the fact that I was famous and, really, my family couldn't cope with it. And what they really thought, because they saw more of me in the papers than in the flesh, was that I didn't give a shit about anybody except myself.

I just got to the stage where I had a nervous breakdown at the beginning of this year, because I felt that I was sitting behind a wall and I could see out and nobody could see in and nobody could see me, and all around me were people saying to me that I didn't give a shit about anybody. Nobody just talks to you about the fucking weather and the price of eggs. And the rift that it caused me within my family made me want to kill myself. I contemplated killing myself on numerous occasions. Because I just couldn't see that there was any way out. But now it's fine and we worked it out because we love each other and love is the thing that wins. Luckily.

SPIN: Why would people say you only care about yourself?

O'CONNOR: Because I escaped. I escaped, that's all. They were still there, and I escaped. I made my dreams come true. My dreams came true, and nobody else's did. And I am a constant reminder to people that they are in pain. And when I talk about these kind of things in public, it upsets people. 'Cause everybody likes to brush everything under the carpet.

SPIN: What dreams have not come true?

O'CONNOR: None. They are all happening.

SPIN: What about men?

O'CONNOR: I don't dream about a man. I don't dream about the things I was brought up to dream about. That's all bullshit, too. That's child abuse, too. You are brought up to believe that a woman is not a complete woman unless she has found a man, et cetera, et cetera, and had children. That's bollocks.

SPIN: You don't feel that way? I don't feel I'm complete without a woman.

O'CONNOR: No. I want to be complete by myself. You can be incomplete with a man. What I'm aiming for is to be a complete person. And if that means a man is with me, great, but I'm not complete because he's with me.

SPIN: I understand that, but I mean it's part of the human experience.

O'CONNOR: Yeah, it is. Of course I want some man to fall madly in love with me and I want to fall madly in love with him, but when it's meant to be it will be and there is nothing I can do about it. In the meantime, my dream is to discover myself.

Because I have no hair, people think I'm angry. And because I speak very directly and have one of those faces that sometimes doesn't express what my feelings are or what my words are—I just look angry or pissed off. But I'm not. I'm an Irish woman. I invite anyone in America to go to Ireland and study Irish women. I am your average Irish woman, particularly your average Dublin woman. We're hard women. We're soft women, as well, but we are hard and we don't fuck around. And we curse a lot.

SPIN: Now, what if you met a man and you fell in love with him and he fell in love with you, and he said, "I love you and adore you, but I saw this picture of you with a wig on and you looked great with hair. How about growing it out?"

O'CONNOR: Then I'd realize he didn't love me at all.

SPIN: No, maybe he really did. It's not a trick question; I'm not trying to trick you.

O'CONNOR: Oh, no, no. I would just think, well, "You can just fuck off then." I mean, if I want to grow my hair—which, in fact, I do want to grow my hair—that's because I want to grow my hair and not because nobody else likes it.

SPIN: Is the intimidation bit somewhat your creation?

O'CONNOR: Nope.

SPIN: Are you sure?

O'CONNOR: Absolutely. It is not a conscious creation. It is because—

SPIN: An unconscious creation?

O'CONNOR: No! It's because I like to wear certain clothes. It's because I like to wear my hair in a certain way and I feel the same as everybody else. But everyone judges a book by its cover. I've always been abused for what I look like.

SPIN: Isn't that why you cut your hair?

O'CONNOR: No. I just refuse to allow it to make me become something else.

SPIN: Do you wake up every day feeling like today you are going to have to defend your position in life?

O'CONNOR: I end up having to do that every day, yeah. In certain situations.

SPIN: Do you want to go to the country for a long weekend and simply not have to deal with what Sinéad O'Connor has to deal with every day?

O'CONNOR: I deal with whatever God gives me to deal with. And I'm more than happy to do that.

SPIN: You really, sincerely believe that, don't you?

O'CONNOR: Yeah. I don't believe that God gives a person more than they can handle.

SPIN: Is the fact that you keep your head shaved   obviously a very conscious act—is that even subconsciously partly be-cause you are a victim? Were a victim?

O'CONNOR: First of all, shaving my head to me was never a conscious thing. I was never making a statement. I just was bored one day and I wanted to shave my head, and that was literally all there was to it. I already had it shaved on the sides and it was about as far as I could go. I think fiddling with the hair is a huge subconscious statement, yeah. Yeah, I suppose it is a subconscious rejection of conformity and of the family and everything that the word *family* can mean. I'm growing it now.

SPIN: Do you have a sense of being a victim?

O'CONNOR: Yeah. I, along with millions and millions of other people, am the victim of a society which aspires to material success in order to fill the emptiness it feels. And as a result of that aspiring, causes a huge pain for people and which results in child abuse. And that's what I'm a victim of, yeah. I'm the victim of a society that doesn't believe in self-expression or fighting for the truth.

SPIN: What do you think is the future of rock 'n' roll?

O'CONNOR: That's very difficult. First of all, you cannot separate music from politics because music has always been the voice of the people. Whether you like the sound of it or not, that's what it is. [*sighs*] God, I think that at the moment the music industry is a microcosm of the world at large. And you can see that in the music industry that its main goals are material and the artists' main goals are material: celebrity, fame, money. That is what they are concerned with, and they drip it in their videos and that is what they say to everybody else. I would like to see that change.

SPIN: Hip-hop is doing it, really, more than anybody.

O'CONNOR: I don't think they do it more than anybody. I think they do it the same amount as heavy metal videos do it.

SPIN: There's more status-symbol consciousness in hip-hop.

O'CONNOR: Yeah, because the Black people are the poorest people in America. And they don't want to live in poverty, and they believe that if they achieve material success that is what it is all about and it just isn't true. And it is an abuse for artists to continue perpetuating that belief.

SPIN: Do you think rock 'n' roll has a viable future?

O'CONNOR: It has dilapidated. You turn on any radio station in the world—all you'll hear is crap. You'll never hear a record. You'll hear entertainment and some of it is very good. But you'll never hear any conscious music. You'll never hear anything that inspires you, that makes you think, that spins you off into a fantasy. You'll never hear that. It has dilapidated.

SPIN: One last question: What's the best Irish joke you've ever heard?

O'CONNOR: Why are Irish jokes so silly?

SPIN: I don't know?

O'CONNOR: So the English can understand them.

GOING IT ALONE

INTERVIEW BY DEIRDRE MULROONEY
"MOTHERS AND BABIES" SUPPLEMENT,
THE IRISH INDEPENDENT
JULY 2004

*Lone parents are much more commonplace nowadays and the
stigma attached to having a baby out of wedlock has largely
lifted. How do single mothers cope during pregnancy and
when rearing their children? Deirdre Mulrooney speaks to
one such woman.*

SINÉAD O'CONNOR, MOTHER TO JAKE (SEVENTEEN YEARS OLD), ROISIN (EIGHT YEARS OLD) AND SHANE (FOUR MONTHS OLD):

I've been a single mother since I was twenty. I suppose because of what I had done for a living in the past, I had a privileged experience. I wasn't materially challenged.

I always wanted to be a mother, but I don't necessarily want to be a wife or a girlfriend. I don't really think the two necessarily have to go together. I never believed in Mr. Right. As a girl, I saw marriage as a death to women. You've to give up your career, your name, everything. I don't believe in that at all. I have a lot of phobias about marriage. I don't want to have to try to be something I'm not and give up my whole personality.

My three children, Jake, Roisin, and Shane, have different fathers and I am very good friends with two of them and in the process of becoming friends with the third one. I believe it's important to put aside any bad stuff that might have gone on between the parents and put the child first.

There were difficulties between my parents, and as a child experiencing that I know it can create an awful split in a child—if the parents are bickering with or about each other or not respecting each other.

Even though I am a single parent, my daughter spends half the time with her father and half with me. Jake's dad lives in England. I did live in England for seventeen years, up until about four years ago. But Jake lived with me the whole time.

Still, his father was always involved in his life.

I wasn't in a relationship with Jake's father but we were very good friends; he was very supportive and he was there at the birth. I lived in his house for six weeks after the baby was born. He was also the only person I knew in England at the time.

I was never in a relationship with Roisin's father as such. We were friends and wanted to have a baby together. He lived in Ireland at the time and I lived in England, so he wasn't really involved in the pregnancy. But he was at the birth. Pretty much from the word go there was a joint custody arrangement. Maybe until Roisin was three it wasn't quite split down the middle.

I went through the last pregnancy without the father's involvement. I had one of my girlfriends there as my birthing partner. It was a great bonding experience for us.

Going through the two pregnancies alone was quite traumatic. Certainly the last one was. It was very difficult emotionally and consequently physically. Not having the support of the father is incredibly painful. I've a lot of terror around childbirth. The [idea] of it was worse than the reality. I had an epidural, though; God, otherwise I would have had a really hard time.

After the birth, I had to build my support network again. During the pregnancy, my main support system was the woman who came with me when I had the [baby].

She and her husband and her family were really supportive, as well as my sister.

I'm really lucky because I have money. I have a woman who does the shopping for me once a week. She fills up the freezer with good food that's already cooked, so the kids get fed if I'm too tired to cook. I also have a woman who comes to tidy up the house three days a week and looks after the baby if I'm tired. My family has been brilliant, as well. You need people to put up with you because you're so hormonal and feel like you're going mad at times. I am very lucky, too, that the three of them have been very easy babies. This baby is an angel.

I have given up work so I don't need child care. I look after the children full-time myself. I just joined the babysitting club www.minderfinders.ie. However, I probably won't start going out much until this baby is a bit older, because if there is the slightest chance that he might smile at me, I don't want to miss it. My eldest is seventeen, so there isn't much looking after there. And the eight-year-old is with her dad half the time. So it's only really very full-on half the time. In December the baby is going to start in a day nursery up the road so I can get back to doing a few things. But I'm really enjoying looking after them full-time: that's why I gave up work.

What I learned with the first baby was that children grow up very fast. I can remember the first time Jake smiled at me as if it was yesterday. When they've all grown up and gone away I'll be bored stupid. So I'll do a lot more things then. Bringing up children is very hard work and you're tired, but the rewards are incredible. They are lovely kids, very happy and affectionate. To see the three of them smiling at you is worth anything.

I think the health system here is brilliant. I was impressed with the health system in England in that the health workers watched you carefully to see you didn't get depressed after having a child. But over here they watch you while you are pregnant for antenatal depression, which I find good because I would be that type that would get depressed while I'm pregnant, not afterwards.

I found the Community Mothers Scheme through the health board very helpful. An older mother comes to you once a month and has a chat with you about what stage your baby is at and gives you advice.

Also the district nurse calls in on you just to make sure that you're okay. The support for people who are vulnerable is great in this country. The health visitors knew that I was having a hard time with the pregnancy, being on my own. It was impressive that they didn't treat me differently to any other person. They really keep their eye on you without being intrusive. The way they handle the single mother issue is brilliant. You know if you were in trouble that they would help you.

I was in a crisis pregnancy with the last one. I wasn't sure which of two guys was the father. One was married and one was not. I wasn't fussed either way because I just love babies.

I remember going to the gynecologist and being ashamed to tell him the situation I was in, and he just laughed. He said there are so many people in this situation that you wouldn't believe it.

I don't think there is much general emotional support for women going through a pregnancy on their own. I'm not ashamed to say I was nearly in the harbour a few times.

I'm sure so were other girls in the same situation. If the guy is not around or you're on your own it's really hard.

I agreed [to] a court order with Roisin's dad to establish what the contact would be. That really helped. For the few years that we didn't trust each other or get on terribly well, we built trust by sticking to what it said on that bit of paper. In a situation where parents have a hard time communicating, it's good to make an agreement and stick to it.

There are days since I've had the new baby that I've been really tired, but that's to be expected. Whether you are single or married you'll get those. Not having to work, it doesn't matter if the baby stays up all night. I just have to get used to the tiredness.

I don't miss work at all. I've just started doing an art class once a week. I need to do something creative just for me. I wouldn't go back to the music business now. When this little one is sixteen, I'll go to college and do a few things. But I'd like to have a few more kids before I get too old.

I'm lucky because my family of origin was unconventional. My father was a bit worried when I got pregnant because I was young, but he wasn't worried because I was a single mother. There was never any attitude from them of "Oh—you don't have a husband." It was more like, "How are you going to look after yourself? Are you going to be able to work?"

The kids are happy with their situation and that's how it has always been. I've never lived with any of their fathers, so they haven't had to deal with any possible trauma associated with that.

I've never experienced any negative attitude towards my being a single mother except one time when I was working in the U.S., when Jake was a baby. TV news reporter Maria Shriver was the only person who ever gave me a hard time about being a single mother and a Catholic.

I love being a mother. I don't know any different. I don't have a minute to be bored. The children are my world and my purpose every day. It's the most creative work I've ever done.

JAH NUH DEAD

INTERVIEW BY NICHOLAS JENNINGS
INSIDE ENTERTAINMENT
JULY 2005

In July 2005, I spoke with Sinéad O'Connor about her reggae album, *Throw Down Your Arms*, that she'd recorded in Jamaica with [musicians] Sly and Robbie. There was a lot going on in the world at the time. Live 8, the series of anti-poverty benefit concerts organized by Bob Geldof on the twentieth anniversary of Live Aid, had just taken place. The news cycle was filled with horrific stories about the suicide attacks by Islamic terrorists that killed fifty-six early-morning commuters on the London Tube. We talked about those events, as well as ganja, God, and her decision never to revisit her pop past again.

But Sinéad was musically motivated—*Throw Down Your Arms* was her first recording since her traditional Irish collection *Sean-Nós Nua*. And she was planning to tour the album. So mostly we focused on her inspiration to record classic roots reggae songs, which she discussed in her typically candid way, with colorful asides about rap music, organized religion, Elton John, and more. She also mentioned her 1992 appearance on TV's *Saturday Night Live* when, following an a cappella performance of Bob Marley's "War," she infamously tore up a photo of the Pope in protest against sexual abuses in the Roman Catholic Church. Here is our conversation.

NICHOLAS JENNINGS: A reggae album from you will be a surprise to most people?

SINÉAD O'CONNOR: People who've been fans of mine for a long time would know that I've been a massive roots fan for years. I make a distinction between roots and reggae. I'm not really a reggae fan at all. But I love roots, which is the religious aspect of reggae music. They would also see the reflection of that within my own music over the years. It's not actually a departure for me because it's something that has had a huge influence on my personality as an artist. I consider myself to be a Rastafarian and have for years. Rasta musicians have had a huge influence on my personality, songwriting, and my vision of what it means to be an artist in these times.

JENNINGS: You've performed with roots musicians?

O'CONNOR: Yes, Burning Spear last year. In the last few months with Bob Andy and Israel Vibrations. I've been to a lot of reggae shows. In the Rasta community they would know me, as far as the whole Pope business, for want of a better description, would have endeared me to numbers of Rasta people. Since those days, I've never played a show anywhere where two Rastas haven't turned up at the dressing room and said, "We want to speak with our sister." There's been a big bond. Obviously, the whole thing about the Bob Marley song on *Saturday Night Live*, which a lot of people don't remember, was that I tied a Rastafarian prayer cloth to the microphone, and the song was a prayer in many ways. Basically that was the point at which I publicly identified myself with Rastafarianism. I've had a very strong bond with those people since I was a child. I was born in December 1966 into what was at that time a Catholic theocracy. In Ireland, the experience of Catholicism has been very different to many other countries. I was born into a country that was a religious dictatorship. Very black-and-white place to be. One of the principal tenets of Catholicism in those days was that to be a good person you have to think that you're shit. I was inspired as a small child by the civil rights movement and the struggle for self-esteem, which existed in descendants of African slaves in America and the Third World. From the time I was three or four, I remember seeing kids being hosed off pavements in America when they tried to go to school, having had to fight for the "right" to go to school. I saw the war that was going on in my own country and the war in Israel. It made me think, even as a child, that God and religion are two very separate things. To me, that's what is attractive about the Rastafarian movement. As an Irish female Catholic survivor of child abuse, I identified enormously with the struggle for self-esteem. One of the first characters who came into my life, which led me into this, was Muhammad Ali. As a child I used to watch him on TV and he was way ahead of his time, shouting about how beautiful he was. To us in Ireland, that was a sin. That's why the kids loved him, because he was saying all the things we weren't allowed to say. It was blasphemy for anyone to declare themselves lovely, let alone a Black man. We began to understand from him and from the freedom movement in America, through Martin Luther King and others, that our struggle was similar to theirs. As a survivor of child abuse I had the same struggle with self-esteem.

As a Catholic woman I had the same struggle with the right to love myself. Or the right to declare myself valid. That's where my identification with these people began. As a teenager, the Black freedom movement, which I prefer to call the movement toward self-esteem, I got into various singers like Curtis Mayfield. He was huge to me. I loved his "We People Are Darker than Blue." That led me to other artists. When I was seventeen, I moved to London. That's when I first came across Rasta people and Rasta music. My manager at the time was Fachtna O'Ceallaigh, who was best friends with a guy who ran a radio station called the Dread Broadcasting Company. This guy ran a store on Portobello Road where he had an open mic session. These young Rastas used to come and sing off the top of their heads these incredible songs. I was quite a religious child. But I observed that God needs to be rescued from religion and that music was one of the ways of doing that. The church of music was quite boring. Once I came across the Rasta people and how they used music to teach scriptures, I found it hugely inspiring. Bringing God alive through music. Since I was a child, I thought that music was one's channel of communication with God. The Rastas were the first I felt that were manifesting that. I learned most of my scriptures from Rasta records.

JENNINGS: Was Bob Marley an early influence?

O'CONNOR: Not really; I didn't get into Bob Marley until later. I bought "Could You Be Loved." But I didn't get mad into him until I was twenty-two-ish. Before that I was into people like Half Pint and The Heptones and Toots and the

Maytals. Most people don't know Bob Marley's hard-core Rasta stuff. It's the more commercial stuff. I only got into Bob Marley when I heard things like "Babylon System." I'm strictly roots. I was into people who saw music as a priesthood. I didn't realize that Bob did until I was older.

JENNINGS: How did you choose the songs for the album?

O'CONNOR: I chose songs that I've lived with for the last twenty years and that have saved my ass. They kept me afloat. "Jah Nuh Dead" by Burning Spear. He's my favorite songwriter. He embodies a wonderful Jamaican trait. He doesn't do small talk. They hardly talk at all. Only when absolutely necessary. Spear can impart an entire world of information in the space of five sentences. He's a very gentle spirit but it's a fantastic art to say a book's worth of stuff in a couple of lines. I did four of his songs. "Marcus Garvey." I was surprised to find that he was very like our own Patrick Pearce, an Irish civil rights fighter. "Y Mas Gan," an Abyssinian tune, is my favorite track on the album. It embodies the whole reason for making the record, the idea that God should be praised continually and that music is the best way of doing that. There's an old Latin saying that he who sings prays twice and the Rastas have had that knowledge for a long time. In these times, no one seems to write religious songs anymore, hymns or anything like that, so we're stuck with the same old boring crap. God must get pretty fed up listening to the boring crap. If I was God and I heard "Y Mas Gan," I'd be like, "Thank me, that's something new." It's a cooler way of making a religious song. "Vampire" has always meant a lot to me. I like the mischief of it and the mischief of Rastafarianism. That's a Lee Perry tune, as is "Curly Locks." "Jah Nuh Dead," "Marcus Garvey," "Door Peep," "He Prayed," and "Throw Down Your Arms" are all Burning Spear. "Prophet Has Arise" is by my favorite band on earth, Israel Vibration. It was very hard to choose one of their songs because I love them so bad. Their album *Same Song* is my favorite album of all time. That's from that album. I had the great joy of singing with them recently at the London Astoria. That was fucking unbelievable. "Downpressor Man" is by Peter Tosh, another favorite songwriter of mine and very underrated in my opinion. These are songs that are normally sung by men. Traditionally, in the roots and reggae arena, women don't sing warrior songs. They sing the love songs. It's quite something for a small woman, let alone a small Irish woman, to try and sing these songs. Especially with Peter Tosh, it's hard to take on the spirit of a nine-foot-tall man. I love the controlled anger of him, the hugeness of his spirit. "Untold Stories" is a Buju Banton song. Of the modern guys I loved Buju and Sizzla. They're both very bad men and believe in terribly bad things. They're very anti-gay. Jamaican culture is very anti-gay. Everyone complains and tries to stop them from playing in England. I don't agree with their position. It makes me sad, but I don't throw the baby out with the bathwater. These guys make great records. I don't believe in everything they believe in. Unfortunately, the slacker the records are the fucking better produced they are. I'm anti-feminist in some ways, although I'm quite feminist really. An album like N.W.A's *Straight Outta Compton* has my favorite track, which is "I Ain't tha 1," which is a real anti-woman song but it's the best fucking song on there.

At the end of the day, you have to feel sorry for someone raised in Jamaican culture to believe those things. Sly and Robbie mixed the album themselves after I left. That was my first time in Jamaica and I went there on my own. I was completely accepted. I had a history with these people before-hand, as far as they were concerned, because of the Pope busi-ness. I wasn't a total stranger. I didn't feel any chauvinism. I thought it might be tricky because I'm a little woman, but it was amazing. It's intimidating to go anywhere on your own as a woman. I didn't buy into the rumors about how danger-ous Kingston is. I just trust in God anyway. Once I got to the studio, it was happy family.

JENNINGS: So with this new album you've returned to work?

O'CONNOR: I wanted to get the muscle going. It seemed the logical follow on from *Sean-Nós Nua*. Once you've tackled those Irish songs as a singer, there's nowhere else for you to go except into religious music. I came out of the mainstream arena and I wish to reenter the arena of religious music. My feeling is that I was in the wrong arena all those years, which is why neither me nor they could understand.

JENNINGS: Can you reconcile the religious arena with com-mercial music?

O'CONNOR: Of course. I'm in an enviable position, which is that I have enough money that I don't have to make re-cords for any other reason than that I love them. That's the only reason, I think, anyone should ever make a record. You shouldn't unless you're going to go crazy if you don't. I'm thirty-eight, nearly thirty-nine, and hopefully I have another thirty-nine years left and I can do what makes me happy and not what I'd do to make money. Obviously, I'm happy to make money though. With this album, I had to get my confidence back up. I hadn't sung a note for three years. I was convinced that I'd forgotten how to sing. Once I started singing again, I started writing songs. I hadn't done that. I had put away all my instruments for three years. Hadn't even looked at a guitar. Now I'm halfway through the next album.

JENNINGS: How different will it be from this one?

O'CONNOR: Extremely different insofar as I've written all the songs and it will be all acoustic. It's called *Theology*. Basically taking all the books from the scriptures and discussing those in songs. A very gentle record. Not hippie dippy corny religious, but quite religious.

JENNINGS: And you'll be performing again?

O'CONNOR: We're going on tour starting in November. I'm beside myself over it.

JENNINGS: What will you perform?

O'CONNOR: It will be just this album and a couple of other things. I came out of the mainstream and I've come back into the religious music arena. There are only two songs that I'm taking with me, therefore, from my former incarnation. "The

Healing Room" (from *Faith and Courage*) and "Thank You for Hearing Me" (from *Universal Mother*). Everything else stays in the past and that's a closed chapter. I don't perform those songs ever.

JENNINGS: And never will?

O'CONNOR: No. I've come out of the pop mainstream arena and I don't want to look back, even artistically. Those songs are about life experiences. I don't want to go back there and that person doesn't exist anymore, as far as I'm concerned, although I have a great fondness for that person. But that's someone who needs to rest in peace. My approach is if I was a new artist starting off. That's how I want to deal with it, as if I've started a new life and this is my first record.

JENNINGS: But your fans will want to hear your old songs?

O'CONNOR: We all need to just really make ourselves happy at the end of the day. I have to put myself first. Some people will go with me and some won't and that's cool. It's very early days in my career and I hope to establish a long and strong career in the religious music arena. I'm trying to do a Mahalia Jackson. A particular transformation has taken place and once that has happened, you can't step backwards. You have to be very sure of who and what you are. I don't want to identify anymore with all of that. I've got to be me. Religious music isn't the best term, it's really religious/spiritual music. But it's about making the distinction that God and religion are two very different things. I'm interested in rescuing God from religion through music. That is my own personal mission of choice.

JENNINGS: Who in the pop arena is making music like that?

O'CONNOR: Mainly in reggae, artists like Sizzla and Buju Banton. Unfortunately, they're also being found with caches of weapons in their front gardens.* Van Morrison, although he's not in the pop arena. There's a guy called Michael Franti, who was with the band Spearhead. They're pretty on course. There's a couple of rappers around, DMX. Some people end up being spiritual without meaning to be. I find 50 Cent quite a spiritual character, although I don't know if he would. Certain records that Eminem has made, "Cleaning Out My Closet," is a hugely spiritualized record, although again he may not realize it. There's an Irish singer, Damien Dempsey, who is the best singer I've heard anywhere. He's on a spiritual journey, I think. With some artists, it doesn't manifest until they're older. I think you'll see more artists switch from the pop arena to the more spiritualized arena. The more successful you become in the pop arena, the more you realize how spiritually bereft it is. Fame and fortune and all that. Patti Smith is another. I don't think in any of the boy band, young girl band. Only when they win awards do they seem to think that God has something to do with this, when actually it's just that someone wanted to make a TV show. Bruce Springsteen of course.

---

*   While both Sizzla and Buju Banton have had run-ins with the law over the years, and Sizzla was arrested then released as part of the 2005 cache find in Kingston to which O'Connor refers, neither has weapons-related convictions (indeed, Banton later had a jail sentence reduced after the firearm possession part was quashed).

JENNINGS: What about Christian artists in pop music like U2 and others?

O'CONNOR: I don't believe in taking on one set of beliefs because you're shutting out all the others. I'll be a whore when it comes to religious studies. I'll be inspired by all of them. It's slightly dangerous to be interested in only one way of looking at God. God doesn't like religion. If you study the books of the prophets, which is the only place where God actually gets a voice, you see the God character in all of the Judaic scriptures, and in most of them he's very troubled by religion. One has to be very careful if you're putting yourself forward as a spiritualized artist that you're not affiliating yourself with one religion or another, because religion and God are very different things. I do believe in Jesus and all the power of Jesus, but that's not all I believe in.

JENNINGS: What's your opinion of Live 8?

O'CONNOR: I think it's incredible what everyone involved did and that includes all the people who went to it. However, I think we have to be very careful about getting into situations where we, if I can crudely put it, are sucking politicians' cocks. We exist to be a voice in the wilderness, which we cease to be if we're having dinner at the White House. I'd be a little wary of that aspect of it. But I think it's amazing what Geldof has pulled off. The sense of power he's given to people so that they feel they can do something. He's not a cocksucker [*laughs*]. He's incredible. You can't help but have immense pride in him as a person and what he's done.

Politicians really use artists. We're hanging out with them so much we forget what we are. We need to keep the boundaries very clear. With Live 8, artists were told not to criticize the war in Iraq. That's the danger. If we end up becoming friends with these people, how can we criticize them? Having said that, I didn't get off my fat arse to do anything for Africa. There are seven deadly sins and one is vanity. And that's a little bugger that will get you if you let it. When Elton John did that song for Diana, turning "Goodbye Norma Jean" into that awful song that perpetuated the myth of Diana as being this confused, crazy, weak woman. That was the establishment's view of her and not the reality. The vanity on the part of the artist allows them to be manipulated by politicians for political purposes. We exist to challenge bullshit, so we mustn't become part of bullshit.

JENNINGS: How would you describe your life right now?

O'CONNOR: I'd characterize it as a rebirth. I'm approaching my work as a new artist and left the past in the past. Sinéad O'Connor is now asleep and something else which is far more nurturing to my soul has come about.

JENNINGS: Is it difficult to get back to singing?

O'CONNOR: Terrifying. A lot of crying. I was absolutely petrified because there's an awful lot to live up to. Everyone considers me such a great singer. But I know the horrible truth. Also, stepping into Kingston with a bunch of guys who've been playing around these records for years and years. That's a little scary. A little woman trying to sing these big man songs. That's a tough task. I cared about it very passionately.

JENNINGS: Did you get any advice from Burning Spear or Israel Vibration?

O'CONNOR: There's a particular kind of handshake that men in Jamaica give each other and traditionally don't give it to women. They grab your hand and you push your right shoulder into the other person's right shoulder. Spear is the only Jamaican man who ever did that to me. That was in New York. He did that handshake with my son and then did it to me. I want to be one of the lads, essentially. That's why I was thrilled Spear did that with me. When you do that handshake, it honors your warrior spirit. To me, part of making this album is honoring the spirit of man. These men are people who have been my guides a lot of my life. I changed the lyric of "Jah Nuh Dead" from "they tried to fool the Black population" to "the whole population" on the grounds that if you got fooled then so did we. Spear wasn't sure about my changing it. It was a little awkward when I told him. A lot of the old-school guys want to make sure you're respecting where they come from. Spear wanted to make sure I got the teachings. Once he understood that I wasn't entirely brainless he was okay with it.

JENNINGS: What are your views on ganja?

O'CONNOR: I support the use of ganja by anybody who wishes to use it. I would use ganja whether I was a Rasta or not. I have been very happily a smoker of ganja since I was twenty and will always be.

JENNINGS: Isn't ganja a sacrament for Rastas?

O'CONNOR: I don't know about that. I'm just a spliff head. I've never partaken it as a sacrament; I've just smoked a lot of joints with Rastas. I haven't done any chalices. Do I condone the use of marijuana? Yes I do. It's not for everyone. I don't drink alcohol. That's not for me. I don't do Class A drugs and I don't condone the use of them at all, except under medical supervision. But when it comes to weed, I think you're better off smoking a joint than having a drink.

JENNINGS: As someone who identifies as a Rasta, will you grow dreads?

O'CONNOR: No, it's a state of mind being a Rasta. It's not about how you look. You don't have to be Black or male or Jamaican or Ethiopian. It's a state of consciousness. Rastafarianism is not a religion; it's a movement. It's about the idea of freeing God from religion. It's a self-esteem movement. It believes, as I do, that religion itself is idolatrous. If you believe that then you can call yourself a Rasta. It's not about how you look but where you're going and what you know. Whether you're part of the team that frees God from religion. Rastafarianism is a school, a set of teachings, lessons, through which you learn that God and religion are two very separate things. I hope you don't mind my going on about God. But we look around the world and dreadful things are happening.

JENNINGS: Like the appalling bombings that just happened in London?

O'CONNOR: Exactly, and people try to solve these things with politics but these are spiritual problems. I know it sounds corny, but there is a fucking God which does respond to the human voice. And no one is calling out, even people who think they believe in it, because they're just talking to the wall which religion told them is God. This world could be fixed up very quickly if people really started discussing these things. So I hope what I'm saying doesn't come across as just another "God is the answer" rant.

SOMETHING BEAUTIFUL

INTERVIEW BY JODY DENBERG
KUTX 98.9 RADIO, AUSTIN, TEXAS
APRIL 11, 2007

JODY DENBERG: You don't have to listen very hard to Sinéad O'Connor's music to hear that spiritual matters have always informed her work. Sinéad's entire twenty years of recordings have dealt with faith and religion in one way or another. Sinéad O'Connor's latest project, *Theology*, is a two-CD set that is the culmination of her musical quest. *Theology* is a word that refers to the study of the nature of God and religious truth. *Theology* is also Sinéad O'Connor's new release, and on it, she explores its title's topic with the songs presented in two ways: once on a disc with sparse acoustic settings, and again on a second disc, which essentially is the same songs given full musical production. I'm Jody Denberg and during the next hour we will talk with Sinéad about this ambitious undertaking and sample many of its songs. Welcome to "'Something Beautiful': The Sinéad O'Connor *Theology* Conversation," and this is the first song from *Theology*. Indeed, it's rightfully called "Something Beautiful."

[Plays "Something Beautiful" by Sinéad O'Connor]

DENBERG: Sinéad O'Connor and the song "Something Beautiful" from her new disc *Theology*, and this is "'Something Beautiful': The Sinéad O'Connor *Theology* Conversation."

Sinéad, it's nice to see you, and I just want to congratulate you on creating such a healing piece of work.

SINÉAD O'CONNOR: Thanks. Thank you.

DENBERG: One of your motivations in recording *Theology* was to make something beautiful, wasn't it?

O'CONNOR: Yeah, that was pretty simply the whole reason for making it. There isn't really any other reason.

DENBERG: Almost sounds like something a child would say to their mom. "I made something; it's beautiful!"

O'CONNOR: Yeah, exactly. That is exactly the spirit in which it's done.

DENBERG: You're creating something beautiful in the midst of a time of war.

O'CONNOR: Hmm.

DENBERG: Sort of a counterbalance to what's going on.

O'CONNOR: Yeah, to me it's really very much an anti-war record, and it's very subtle. But that is what it is. It's a reaction, I suppose, to seeing theologies being misinterpreted and used as weapons, if you like. And not to name any particular religion, but you know, the war that we see going on right now is happening purely because some people interpreted a particular theology in a particular way. So, I suppose it's my response to that. I suppose there's a school of thought that one cannot solve political problems—or spiritual problems rather—with politics; that the problems that we see in the world are not political but, in fact, spiritual. To try and solve them with politics is like throwing water in a hole of a sinking boat. At some point we have to actually go back to the question of spirituality if we want to make the world a good place, you know.

DENBERG: I heard you say that since you were seven years of age, you thought about making this record. How so?

O'CONNOR: Yeah, I guess because I grew up on a very tiny island, which is called Ireland, which at the time was a theocracy in both the negative and positive suggestions of the word. A very religious country. Also, a very musical country with a tradition of singing. I was one of the people that was affected very positively by Catholicism, actually, and by the religiosity of the country. And I'm rare in that. But I also was involved from a very young age in singing a lot of the religious songs, like in choirs or even just at home. My father was a singer, and my mother also was a singer, not for a living, you know; it's not what they did for a living, but it was their love. There was music everywhere, all kinds of music in my house. All kinds of anything to do with music, and a vast selection of genres that my parents were into. Like from John Lennon to *Oklahoma*, you know what I mean, but I got involved at a very young age in the school choirs, and that's where I fell in love with the religious songs, like, from the age of six and seven, so it was since then that I wanted to kind of be able to write those kind of songs.

DENBERG: The version of the song "Something Beautiful" that we just heard a few minutes ago was from the London sessions disc of *Theology*. Why did you decide to record these songs both in London; those sessions were fully produced instrumentally, but you also did a version in Dublin in an acoustic setting, and on *Theology*, each session has its own disc.

O'CONNOR: I guess it was an accident that happened. Originally, I wanted to make an acoustic record because from years of doing shows, I had noticed that when I go at the end of each show to do fifteen or twenty minutes with just acoustic guitar, the audience really loved that part and responded to it. So, I was figuring for a long time that my own hardcore audience would love an acoustic album, so I had started to commission a guy to work on that, and started to work on it, and paid the first thirty grand, and then what happened was Ron Tom, who's produced the London sessions, tracked me down and rang me and said that he really wanted to work with me. So, I went over to London to make some demos with him, but the only songs I had were these songs. I hadn't written any others. So, we demoed them, but as far as I was concerned it was just to see how we got on working together—see what it sounded like. But if I was gonna work on an album with him it would be the next album. Only, he begged me basically to let him do this album. Like, literally on his knees, nearly crying, he said to me his life would just not be worth living if I didn't let him do it, you know. So, I decided to keep—to do the two albums. And what I did is, I didn't tell the guys in Dublin about the London one, and I never let Ron hear the Dublin one, either. None of them knew anything about what was going on, on either side. So, that was fun, although I was waiting for the guys in Ireland to kill me when they found out.

DENBERG: Are they okay with it now?

O'CONNOR: Yeah, they were a bit freaked out at first, which I knew they would be. But then they were okay. Once they saw how vastly different it was, they were okay with it.

DENBERG: The next song we're about to hear from *Theology* is from the Dublin sessions. And the album's primarily comprised of your new original compositions, but there's a few covers. We're about to listen to a song written by the great Curtis Mayfield, "We People Who Are Darker than Blue." How does this song fit into the *Theology* project for you?

O'CONNOR: In a way it's a kind of a red herring; it does and it doesn't fit. It fits in my own theology because I would see Curtis as a prophet, really, and I'm very fascinated with the prophets and with the books of the prophets. The idea of how these books were written thousands of years ago but really applied to nowadays. But I think that Curtis had similar blood in him in that he was writing about things that were going on in his time, but actually they apply probably more so now in our time. To me there are links between this war that's going on and the escalation of violence among teenagers. You could say that people like George Bush or Tony Blair, that they're father figures, actually—that they're the fathers of their nations, and they condone the use of violence as a way of sorting things. Of course, that's what the children are going to do. So, to me, that's part of why I included that song, also. It's a call to be more than society says you can be. And so, for me, also on a personal level of why I did that song, was really to talk to myself about my own sense of unworthiness of making a record like this, or my own sense of feeling useless or feeling the—I identify also with the racism thing because I feel that the prejudice about famous people is a similar thing, and particularly the Sinéad O'Connor thing, that I'd be dealing with a lot of prejudice about who I am or—that can really cause a lot of self-esteem problems, as well. It can kinda make you just feel like, what's the point. In a way, that song was an encouragement to myself, actually, not to stand around this town and let what others say come true because I'm not good-for-nothing. So, it's that kind of thing as well, a kick up one's own ass.

[Plays "We People Who Are Darker than Blue" by Sinéad O'Connor]

DENBERG: "We People Who Are Darker than Blue," a Curtis Mayfield song performed by Sinéad O'Connor from her new two-CD set *Theology*. Of course, people who are darker than blue refers to people of color, but I also heard it as blue as a mood.

O'CONNOR: Yeah, me too. That's how I hear it—people who are very, very sad.

DENBERG: Did growing up in Ireland with all the strife make you spiritually introspective at a young age?

O'CONNOR: Yeah, you know, I'm convinced I can remember my baptism. I'm sure probably I'm wrong, but I'm almost certain that I can remember my baptism, and that I remember understanding what it meant. The Ireland of those days was one where all there was was religion. You went into anyone's house, it was covered in pictures of the Pope and pictures of saints, those Sacred Heart lamps. Every family was extremely religious, and Catholicism was the main religion. Also, another thing was that I was born on a particular day, which was the 8th of December, which is a big Catholic feast day. It's the Feast of the Immaculate Conception. But if you're a girl born on that day, it's associated with the Virgin Mary. So, because I was a girl born on that day, everyone would always give me Virgin Mary things. That's what happens if you're born on that day; if you're a girl, you're always associated with the Virgin Mary. You couldn't get away from that kind of introspection really.

DENBERG: You were ordained several years ago in the Latin Tridentine Church as Mother Bernadette Mary. Is that a path that you still follow?

O'CONNOR: Yeah, very much so. I would see music as my priesthood. I mean that's what I think this record is, the act of a priest actually.

DENBERG: But then in 2003, you announced your retirement from music. Was it shortly after that that you began studying scripture at a college in Dublin?

O'CONNOR: Yeah, it probably was shortly after that. Now, I'd been studying all my life, actually, just privately; I'd been reading theology all my life, again, since I was young. I started to study Judaic theology when I was like nine or ten. Over the years [I've] studied a lot of theologies just by myself on the Internet or buying books. But the first time I went to college was 2003. I started to study Kabbalah years ago when I was about nineteen, as well.

DENBERG: One of your new songs that we're just about to hear from the London sessions is inspired by Psalm 33. Let's give it a listen, then we'll talk about it. From her new double-disc set *Theology*, this is Sinéad O'Connor with "33."

[Plays "33" by Sinéad O'Connor]

DENBERG: Welcome back to "'Something Beautiful': The Sinéad O'Connor *Theology* Conversation." Sinéad, the last song we heard, "33," was inspired by Psalm 33. I'm not familiar with it, but the lyrics spoke to me about the power of music to bring about spiritual transformation.

O'CONNOR: That's very true, but it's also about the spoken word. The first word of it is *sing*; it gives an instruction. It's really about the power of the spoken word. Also, the power of music, but specifically with the use of the human voice, and that's a kind of a theme in many theologies. Most theologies have, at the beginning of them, the declaration, somehow, that God either spoke or sang the world into existence. That, if you look at it in the beginning, was the word, the same in the Hindu, I can't remember what it is, but the Hindu religion. The Māori culture believe that God sang the world into existence.

DENBERG: While you were studying scripture recently, was there a point where you realized you wanted to make music again, and that you wanted to express what you were learning?

O'CONNOR: What happened was I stopped working in 2003 and, to be honest, I hadn't worked a whole lot before that for a few years, and I had been focusing full-time on my kids for about six years before that. I had released *Sean-Nós Nua*, which was a traditional Irish record, but I had only worked a miniscule amount. I had come out of the rock and pop arena, really, before I retired. And then what happened was I began to really feel the need to go to work again because in music, especially, your work is your social life really, so you're not working, you're sitting on your tod. I couldn't bear the sight of the supermarket once more, either. I did it for six years full-on by myself kind of thing, and it's great, but like my kids began to beg me to go to work because they hate my cooking, as well.

But I thought to myself, "How can I work in music?" because if you have such a thing inside you, you'd be depressed if you weren't using it. It would start to work against you. And so, I'd ask myself, "How can I work in music in a way that isn't gonna mess me up?" because I do find the rock and roll arena a very hard place to cope with. It's not conducive to my nature. A lot of ass-kissing. I find that very difficult to do, and so I've always been a square peg in a round hole in that arena, which is why I kept getting in trouble every time I opened my mouth. I can't be something I'm not, either. I had this counselor for a while, and she said, "Well the thing to do is stick with the knitting," as she put it. So I thought, "Well, how can I stick with the knitting?" So she said, "Well, sticking with the knit-ting means you go back to the reason why you're doing the thing in the first place," and I remember the reason is, when I was seven or eight, I wanted to make religious records, actu-ally. And, somehow, as a teenager, I got caught up with the, "Oh, I want to get laid," and I made pop records so guys will want to shag me. That's the way it works when you're a teen-ager, you know. So, now, it just began to dawn on me that I could work in a different arena which would actually nurture me, rather than feed on me. I'm aware I wouldn't be a square peg in a round hole, although I suspect I'll get in trouble in that arena, too, because you have to be really good, don't you, in that arena, but I'm not really good, but I think that arena needs people who are not really good.

DENBERG: Well, sometimes, quote, unquote, religious music, it can be a little hokey.

O'CONNOR: Exactly, yeah.

DENBERG: And how did you, I mean, were you concerned about how to express yourself in a way that wouldn't be self-righteous or corny?

O'CONNOR: Yeah, I was very concerned, and my mantra during the making of the record was that there is a fine line between corny and cool, when you really want to stay on the right side of the line. That's why I stayed away from the New Testament, actually. Not that I don't believe in Jesus and everything, because I do, but if you start going on about Jesus you put people off, and it's kinda not cool. So, there was really a concerted effort not to be uncool.

DENBERG: We're about to hear the Dublin sessions version of your song "Dark I Am Yet Lovely." Again, the notion of darkness. This piece is inspired by the Song of Songs. Is it saying that the only true love is the love of God?

O'CONNOR: Well, what I love about this is that there's certain theologies, Hinduism is one, where God is allowed to be female. The God characters are allowed to be female, and in Judaism, they used to allow for the idea of God the mother, also. And the idea of God the mother is a very hotly debated and sore point in Catholicism. And in lots of religions in the old, old days, the idea of God the mother was acceptable. What I love about this song is that its theology is the female character is actually God.

[Plays "Dark I Am Yet Lovely" by Sinéad O'Connor]

DENBERG: "Dark I Am Yet Lovely," the Dublin sessions version of a new Sinéad O'Connor song from her new album *Theology*. Sinéad, you were saying that raising your family kept you from writing. I say this with no moral judgment whatsoever, but you have four children from four different fathers. Your oldest is about eighteen and you just had a new baby in December?

O'CONNOR: Yeah, yeah.

DENBERG: Does your specific domestic situation have any special advantages or disadvantages?

O'CONNOR: Well, it makes Father's Day very busy, you know, which is an advantage. I don't know; I never think about it 'cause to me it's normal, so I don't really think about it. It's just our normality and everybody gets on well.

DENBERG: During the time you were taking a break, did your earliest musical successes support you and your family when you weren't working?

O'CONNOR: Yeah. Very much so, yeah. Very much so.

DENBERG: Years ago, you did your version of "Don't Cry for Me Argentina." Andrew Lloyd Webber and Tim Rice, they said it was the definitive version of that *Evita* anthem. Is that part of what led you back to their songbook? Because you do a version, on this new album, of "I Don't Know How to Love Him," which they wrote, which is from the play *Jesus Christ Superstar.*

O'CONNOR: I know. The reason I did that song is, I remember that coming out when I was probably about five. Let me see, I was born in '66, and I think it came out in '74. I was, what, maybe seven or eight, is it? And I remember hearing that song and saying at that time, "That's my song. That is so my song. They have written that song for me, like, to do." So, I was passionate about the song. I hated the musical. I hated every other song. Couldn't stand it. I found it very corny and embarrassing and awful. But I loved "I Don't Know How to Love Him." I always wanted to record that song at some point, and obviously this was the place to do it. I had a letter from Tim Rice recently, again, saying that this was the definitive version of that song. And, what did he say? Which I thought was a magical thing to say, that this song has been a part of his life for forty years and he wrote it, but he has now heard things in it that he never heard before. Which, I think, is incredible, if you can make a songwriter hear stuff in his own song that he didn't hear before. So, I'm happy with that.

[*Plays a piece of "I Don't Know How to Love Him" by Sinéad O'Connor*]

DENBERG: The song originally heard in the play *Jesus Christ Superstar*, that was "I Don't Know How to Love Him" performed by Sinéad O'Connor from her new CD *Theology*.

That's the only song on *Theology* that you don't perform acoustically as well as with the production.

O'CONNOR: Yeah, yeah. Because the acoustic album was finished before we got to the point of recording. Actually, "I Don't Know How to Love Him" was a last-minute thing. I had, when I heard it, always wanted to do it, but I didn't think of it for this record because, actually, I didn't want to do anything New Testament for this record; I wanted it to be strictly Old Testament.

DENBERG: It's such a loving and compassionate song. There really isn't an aggressive attitude on *Theology*.

O'CONNOR: No, deliberately, because it's an anti-war record, and my thing is, look, these wars are happening because of theology, 'cause of how people on both sides interpret theology, or on all three sides, should I say. And my thing is, therefore, let's argue people on their own theology. Because you can argue against what they're saying on their own theology, you know. And so, it was very important to me not to have anything slightly bitter or slightly aggressive, and to be able to show that the God character is, in fact, anti-war and anti-violence.

DENBERG: But, you say, on this album, there's no message, no preaching, just love, spirituality, reconciliation, knowledge. Has your life's path led you to this more peaceful place?

O'CONNOR: Yeah, very much so. And, I mean, music is the thing that leads me. This music would have led me to that place, also.

DENBERG: A lot of people remember, about fifteen years ago, you tore up a photograph of the Pope on American television in protest of child abuse in Irish Catholic schools. So, with all that you've experienced since then, and all the studying that you've done, do you have any regrets about doing that?

O'CONNOR: No, not at all. I had done all the studying before that. That's why I did it. I don't have any regrets about that, no. But it's not something that—what's the word—my own people are always on at me to explain it, but I don't think I need to be understood.

[Plays "Whomsoever Dwells" by Sinéad O'Connor]

DENBERG: Sinéad O'Connor and the Dublin sessions version of "Whomsoever Dwells" that's from her two-CD set *Theology.* Sinéad, "Whomsoever Dwells" was inspired by Psalm 91. What is that psalm, or that psalm's meaning to you?

O'CONNOR: Well, that single psalm has been with me, really, since I was about eighteen years of age when I was first introduced to it. My first album took its title from that psalm; I had someone read a section of that psalm on it. And, with this psalm as one of the most magical or powerful psalms, there's obviously—it's a protection. The idea is that absolutely nothing can happen to you if you state this psalm in a particular situation. Or, even if you just think it. And there's a power in this psalm that would stop a bullet, literally, if you believed it. It's also a psalm which is used in psychic development, a person who wanted to develop their psychic capacities; for example, if they said that every day, they would find that their capacity increases. Or, if you're a frightened and anxious kind of person, if you said that every day, you would begin to become less anxious. It's always been a magical and powerful psalm to me, and kind of expresses the way I feel about the God thing—that it's a massive protector, and that nothing can actually harm you if you're dealing with that.

DENBERG: With all these various studies that you've done, do you consider yourself a member of any religion?

O'CONNOR: Catholic by birth and culture. That's how I consider it. But I am inspired by lots of other religions, if you like.

DENBERG: The song we just heard, "Whomsoever Dwells," and many of the songs here sing of Jah. Does an interest in Rastafarianism jibe with an interest in the Old Testament?

O'CONNOR: The Rastafarian movement is an Old Testament prophetic movement. It's not a religion. That's quite an important thing for people to understand. It's an Old Testament prophetic movement whose raison d'être, if you like, is to remind religion that there is a God. And . . . which needs to happen.

DENBERG: Most of us, we just know the word *Jah* from great reggae songs.

O'CONNOR: Yeah, well, *Jah* was a Jewish word before it was a Rasta word. The Rastafarian movement is what you'd call Judeo-Christian. So they're, you know, sorta half Jew, half Christian.

DENBERG: Perhaps the hardest-hitting song on *Theology* is this one, "The Glory of Jah." It was inspired by the prophet Samuel?

O'CONNOR: Yeah. Yeah.

DENBERG: Let's listen to that one.

[Plays "The Glory of Jah" by Sinéad O'Connor]

DENBERG: Wow. Sinéad, it's been enlightening to talk to you during this past hour about the new project *Theology* and to hear this new music with such peace and purity at its core. I know for a while you stopped talking to the press altogether, and it seemed for years that the media, they liked to talk about your hair or your sexuality or other tabloid stuff. Did that frustration lead to you having a silence with the press?

O'CONNOR: Well, I guess that's why I retired really, in that I wanted to get back and find a sense of myself as an ordinary person, and find out who I am as opposed to what this image of me was that was being portrayed by media, even to me. And, you know, my experience of doing interviews was that, nine times out of ten, people really want to treat you badly and ask you a lot of prejudice and misrepresent you, to the point where you end up depressed; you end up wanting to kill yourself. I was literally suicidal for some years. So many people were getting the wrong end of the stick about me altogether, and wanted the wrong end of the stick, and didn't want to actually see things the right way. I really needed to come away from that and find my value because it was a really desperate situation I felt I was in.

DENBERG: But yet you have in the past and, once again, are using your platform of celebrity to stand for something.

O'CONNOR: Yeah.

DENBERG: Were there any specific artists or people who inspired this approach in you?

O'CONNOR: Well, all my life, the first voice that I remember hearing, as a baby—and I remember being a baby; babies experience the world through their ears. They can't see anything, they're just lying around, they don't know what's going on, they hear things. And the first thing I remember hearing was John Lennon. The next thing I remember hearing is Johnny Cash. Right? All the people that my mother and my father were listening to, they were all protest singers. I grew up going, "Aye," and we were listening to musicals and everything else, as well, but the chief, big capitals were the guys that were actually standing for something, and they weren't just singing so they could be famous and meet loads of girls—although I'm sure that was a side—but, you know what I mean, they stood for something. And they showed that. John Lennon in particular was someone who showed that, if you could, you should use your platform as much as you possibly can for the sake of good.

DENBERG: And you were born on the day that John Lennon died.

O'CONNOR: Yeah.

DENBERG: And you've been making music for twenty years, and you just turned forty by the way. Happy Birthday.

O'CONNOR: Yeah, thanks.

DENBERG: We're going to conclude with the Dublin sessions version of the reggae spiritual "Rivers of Babylon." You surprised us here because you added some additional lyrics.

O'CONNOR: Yeah. Well, again, I, on the record, I wanted no violence or bitterness. The purpose of the record was to make a peaceful place and to show that. I always wanted to write a book of theology, but I can't write books, right? So I've done it with the record. And my own theology would be wanting to show that the God character is actually a very soft and gentle and compassionate and peaceful character. So, when you look at the words of the "Rivers of Babylon" they're kind of bitter, and also, I can't identify with it. I was never taken away and carried into captivity. But, also, what I didn't like is that I used to sing that song in choirs when I was a kid and I was really moved by it. I loved it every time, and still do, every time I either hear it or sing it. What I felt was there was a way in church where people would say prayers, it was boring and monotone. You know, *duh duh duh duh duh duh duh*. Well, the same was happening with "Rivers of Babylon," when it got to the "Then the wicked carried us away," because no one in my culture could identify with it; they'd sing it really boring, do you know what I mean? They'd sing it like it meant nothing. To me, that song now, or the way I've written it, is about why did I retire? Also, I broke my guitar because my tour managers required songs. That's the intention.

[Plays "Rivers of Babylon" by Sinéad O'Connor]

DENBERG: That was Sinéad O'Connor's singular version of "Rivers of Babylon." It comes from her new two-CD set *Theology*, which reveals that, for all her stylistic twists and turns over the years, Sinéad's body of work has a spiritual continuity—works at once inspirational and empowering. I'm Jody Denberg, and I hope you enjoyed "'Something Beautiful': The Sinéad O'Connor *Theology* Conversation." Sincere thanks to Chuck Oliner and all at Koch Records, to you for listening, and especially to Sinéad for her courage and beauty. Thank you, Sinéad.

O'CONNOR: Thanks. Thank you.

HOW ABOUT I BE ME (AND YOU BE YOU)?

INTERVIEW BY CHRIS AZZOPARDI
PRIDE SOURCE
JULY 22, 2014

In 1992, Sinéad O'Connor was at the height of her career following the success of "Nothing Compares 2 U" when, during a one-woman protest against sexual abuse in the Catholic Church, she tore up a pic of Pope John Paul II on *Saturday Night Live*. Causing an uproar, and eventually thwarting her pop-culture presence (not that she cared), that defiance would come to define the Irish singer's life and career.

Over twenty years later, O'Connor found herself entangled in more controversy—this time with Miley Cyrus, who became the target of the Grammy winner's digs last year. The two famously feuded in 2013 over the music business, when Sinéad warned the twerker that it "will prostitute you for all you are worth" (per O'Connor's people, questions about the viral brawl were off-limits for this interview).

Does Sinéad have balls? Of course she does. Big ones. She talked about that region during our recent conversation, insisting that sex—whether it's with a man or a woman—isn't necessary for making her "dick hard." Still, she lets it all hang out on her tenth studio album, *I'm Not Bossy, I'm the Boss* (out August 12), candidly revealing that, "Everybody wants something from me / They rarely ever wanna just know me."

The exception: this chat, during which Sinéad recalled her introduction to the gay community—and how that community gave her the courage to be herself, speak out and "take shit."

CHRIS AZZOPARDI: With regard to this album and your last, *How About I Be Me (And You Be You)?*, released in 2012, you've been on a mission to find yourself. What kind of sacrifices and choices did you have to make on that journey to self-actualization?

SINÉAD O'CONNOR: Gosh, God, I don't know. I suppose it's the same for everybody. It's not like you're suddenly there and you don't have any more work to do; it's a life's work for all of us, isn't it? It doesn't finish until you get to the other side. I think, actually, the things that help you self-actualize are the mistakes—so-called mistakes. I don't like that word. But the things that you get wrong is how you learn to get things right.

AZZOPARDI: The album's lead single, "Take Me to Church," seems partly inspired by redemption. What mistake in your life was the turning point for you?

O'CONNOR: In terms of the song, I suppose the whole album really is a set of love songs. They're all romantic songs, and there are a number of characters on the record—three or four different female characters, one of whom turns up a lot more than the others—and there's a certain journey that that character is taking throughout the record. In a way, that's the answer to the question.

The character is someone who believed all her life that somehow a relationship would make everything wonderful, and that glorious man or woman would come along and carry her into the sunset, that everything would be wonderful. Those of us who have been wounded growing up want to create in our adulthood some perfect family situation or perfect romantic situation that we think will give us something back that we wish we had—that can mean we project onto people romantically. You can tell yourself that someone is just the most perfect, wonderful, glorious, la la la la, and they can be the most awful asshole that ever walked the face of the earth—and so could you! [*laughs*]

The song is more about the idea of romance, and on the whole album that character in particular takes a journey through being a romantic—a pedestal-putting-upon type of a character—who matures when she sees the reality of the situation as opposed to the illusion. I don't know if that answers the question properly, but I think that's the point at which you can understand yourself—when you see the reality of your situation as opposed to what you want to see, the illusions we all want to see.

AZZOPARDI: It's no secret that you have a history with the Catholic Church. So knowing that, and also being a gay man who grew up Catholic, I can't help but listen to "Take Me to Church" and think it's more than just a song about romance.

O'CONNOR: The song actually isn't about the church at all. I don't explain what songs are about because I don't think you should. I think you take away from the audience the experience of being able to imagine it's about them, so I shouldn't actually tell you what "Take Me to Church" is about—the reason you like it is because of what it means to you. But to me, the church in the song symbolizes relationships. It's a reference back to that old song from *My Fair Lady*, "Get Me to the Church on Time," where the father of Audrey Hepburn's character is getting married, and I'm trying to reference that song in my own song, where, really, the character is talking about relationships.

This is a person who, perhaps, has gotten very depressed about a particular relationship not working out because they completely idolize this person, but this person has turned out to be somebody frightening and not someone who could keep the character safe. It's the, "Oh, I want to die because he or she doesn't love me." The character is standing there with the rope around their neck about to jump off a tree and says, "Oh, now hold on, this asshole isn't worth it. Actually, I'm fucking great, and what am I thinking?" So that moment—it's not something that I've been through, but it's something I suppose I can understand when I've been with other people. It's that moment of understanding that actually you're perfectly all right without this person that you've completely idolized and imagined as the most wonderful creature on earth. She understands in that moment that love has to be safe.

AZZOPARDI: Suicide comes up on another song from this album, "8 Good Reasons," except it sounds like it's coming from a more personal place.

O'CONNOR: Yeah, "8 Good Reasons" and "How About I Be Me" would be the most autobiographical songs on this record.

AZZOPARDI: What are the "eight good reasons" that kept you alive when you almost took your own life? I imagine a few of them were your children.

O'CONNOR: They are my children's eyes.

AZZOPARDI: During that song, you also hint toward a possible ninth reason. What would that be?

O'CONNOR: Well . . . that's a secret.

AZZOPARDI: "I became the stranger no one sees"—that lyric seems especially telling. With that line, what are you reflecting on? When in your life have you felt invisible, like an outsider?

O'CONNOR: Let me see . . . I'm trying to find the best way to answer this. Yeah, there would be times that you are invisible—for the most part you are invisible, except when you're making music. It's really a song about being in the music business and the effects the music business—the business part of it—can have on you. It's not about the things that life does to you. There was nothing in my life apart from my job that ever made me want to run for the window. [*laughs*] I can actually laugh about it now, thank God, but it's . . . I've lost my train of thought now. I've forgotten, really, what you've asked me. I suppose it's a delicate subject.

AZZOPARDI: In your life and in your career, have you felt invisible?

O'CONNOR: Oh yeah. It's a very complicated thing to explain, but the price you pay for being a successful musician is your life, and the more successful you are, the more of a price you pay. That makes you invisible. People project onto you, and they see something that isn't really you, and the only time you're with people who are relating to you and who you really are is when you're with your family or friends, or when you're making music. The business of music is a really ugly business, and it's difficult that the price you pay metaphorically for being successful is your life.

AZZOPARDI: Do you feel like yourself more now than ever?

O'CONNOR: Yeah, I do—certainly musically. I wasn't comfortable when I was younger for a myriad of reasons, but now I am very comfortable with who I am as a musician.

AZZOPARDI: The LGBT community can certainly empathize with the struggle to be comfortable with who you are. When was the first time you felt a connection to gay people in your life?

O'CONNOR: I grew up in Ireland and there was no such thing as "gay" in the seventies. I had never even heard of "gay," except for there was a female impersonator who had a big TV show in the seventies, a guy called Danny La Rue. I used to love his show, but I never knew there was any such thing as gay until I was seventeen.

I moved to London and I had a totally straight but cross-dressing cousin who brought me to all these clubs in London. Hippodrome Nightclub & Disco was the first I went to, and it was full of guys dressed up as the most beautiful looking women—way more beautiful than any other woman was ever gonna hope to look! I thought that was incredible, and then I went to Kensington Market, and I thought, "Jesus, England is the greatest country on earth!" They were selling red stilettos—size 12!—and I was like, "Oh my God, that's the coolest thing ever," as far as I was concerned, because I had come from a completely sexually repressed place—repressed in every way, you know? So I had actually never heard of any such thing as gay until I went to the Hippodrome, and put it this way, I was really jealous that I was never gonna look that fucking good.

But in all seriousness, I'll never forget that moment, walking into that toilet in the Hippodrome and it being a real sort of glamorous scene—real posh toilet, all fluffed up mirrors and cushions like a boudoir type of place. In the country that I came from, you couldn't be you in any way at all. No one could've walked down the street dressed like those guys were. You'd have the shit kicked out of you, and not just for that, but a girl like me would have the shit kicked out of her if she walked around with a short skirt, if you expressed anything different at all. So it was real inspiring to me to see those guys able to walk around and be who they were. I actually find the whole gay community an enormous inspiration to me because, Jesus, I've never taken the kind of shit gay people take.

AZZOPARDI: But you've taken a fair amount of shit.

O'CONNOR: No, I know, but I suppose in a way what I'm trying to say is that it's easier to take shit when you are inspired by people such as those in the gay community. Because if a guy is brave enough to walk around dressed up as a woman—if a man is prepared to do that—as far as I'm concerned, any of us can fucking do anything. I just admire that so fucking much.

AZZOPARDI: You told *Entertainment Weekly* in 2005, "I'm three-quarters heterosexual, a quarter gay." What fraction of you is gay these days?

O'CONNOR: I'm forty-seven years of age and I hope, like the character on the record, that I've matured somewhat. Here's the thing: I think if you fall in love with someone, you fall in love with someone and I don't think it would matter what they were. They could be green, white and orange, they could be whatever the opposite of gay or straight is. I don't believe in labels of any kind, put it that way. If I fall in love with someone, I wouldn't give a shit if they were a man or a woman.

AZZOPARDI: I can't say the same for myself, because I'm just not into the lady bits.

O'CONNOR: Obviously, yeah. What I'm trying to say is, I'm old enough not to be going by my dick. It's not about what gets my dick hard or not. I'm old enough for that to not be the point. But I think maybe females are different—what makes us want to have sex with someone is that we like their personality. Guys, whether they're gay or straight, you all just like to fuck and think later. [*laughs*]

AZZOPARDI: When you look out currently at the next generation of artists, what do you see? Who inspires you?

O'CONNOR: I'm old-fashioned in that I'm not necessarily terribly inspired by anything that I hear on the radio that's getting made nowadays, and that's partly because I don't bother my arse, which is terrible and inexcusable. I'm so addicted to the kind of music that I like, which is pretty much Chicago blues. I don't hear anything on the radio that gets me as excited as that. Yeah, so I guess I'm a fuddy-duddy. There's nothing. Well, Adele, obviously, she's very inspiring. Amy Winehouse to me was extraordinary, as is Adele. I miss Amy Winehouse enormously; the bar was raised terribly high when she stepped in. I don't know, though . . . I'm inexcusably uneducated as to what's going on now.

AZZOPARDI: Are you out of touch with pop culture by choice?

O'CONNOR: It's just that when I happen to be driving around in the car and hear any of it, it's boring to me. I'm not saying that that's a judgment on it—it's as much a judgment on me, perhaps. I just can't find anything that's as exciting as Chicago blues to me. It used to be that people used real instruments, made real music and wrote real songs about real things. People stood up in their jeans and T-shirts and moved people.

AZZOPARDI: When you initially shaved your head, you were making a statement—you were protesting the objectification of women. What does that symbol of identity and empowerment mean to you now?

O'CONNOR: I guess it just means "me." You know, (for the cover of *I'm Not Bossy, I'm the Boss*) I ventured into the latex and wig territory there for the laugh, and there's been quite a desire on the part of some people that I might continue down that line, but I'm quite pleased that I look the way that I look, and I guess I associate the hairdo with me. I don't feel like me if I don't have my head shaved. And yeah, it does mean, too, I can put on a dress and I'm still not selling what everyone else wants me to sell.

THE LAST INTERVIEW: PROTEST SINGER

THE VIEW
AMERICAN BROADCASTING COMPANY
JUNE 25, 2021

JOY BEHAR: Well, that was singer-songwriter Sinéad O'Connor performing her 1990 hit ballad "Nothing Compares 2 U." Never a stranger to controversy—well, then, she's come to the right show. Sinéad is back in the spotlight with an unapologetic new memoir called *Rememberings*, so please welcome the talented and always outspoken Sinéad O'Connor.

Welcome to the show Sinéad, lovely, lovely, lovely to have you here.

SINÉAD O'CONNOR: Hi, thank you so much, I've always wanted to do this show, thank you!

BEHAR: You're a wonderful talent. So, in your new book, you reveal a lot of personal and shocking and emotional moments in your life and your career. You said, "I feel the only reason God gave me my career at all was to write this book." So, can you give us your thoughts on that, on that idea, what you said. What do you mean?

O'CONNOR: Well yeah, I guess, not to get too heavy, but you know Ireland under the theocracy was a very difficult place for children to be. And while there have been a ton of reports done on the sexual abuse scandal and the whole thing, there's never been a report done on what went on in people's houses as far as child abuse was concerned. And so, myself and my siblings, growing up, you know, what we were going through, when I was quite small, I made the decision in my mind to make sure that I told the whole universe what happened, because otherwise, we could have died in the house and nobody would have known. And as I'm saying that, I'm speaking for probably half the population of Ireland, you know. It was a massive issue, child abuse, the product of the theocracy manifested—the whole thing manifested itself in the form of all kinds of child abuse. And, yeah, I guess as I say, I wanted to make sure. A bit like the Ken Burns documentary where they're talking about Vietnam? Some of the soldiers are saying what they found most difficult about it was that they couldn't find any meaning for it, they couldn't transcend it, consequently. My thing was to tell it so as to transcend it, so I always say the book is actually the most important song I ever wrote.

MEGHAN MCCAIN: That's really beautiful. You signed your first record deal at eighteen years old and you were nominated for Grammy awards for your first two albums. You're obviously a huge star, and in the book, you write about how record executives told you that you needed to look more feminine with longer hair and dresses. You said all of this led you to shave your head and obviously not wear dresses. Tell us about all of that, please.

O'CONNOR: Well, I think it's a funny chapter, I hope, in the book. I think I wrote it so that it's amusing. The whole chapter of getting the haircut was quite funny, but yeah, that was the eighties, you know; geez, that was the least of what was going on. You were running away from record executives the whole time and pulling your skirt down. But yeah, they summoned me to lunch one day and I had a bit of a mohican, and they asked me would I grow my hair and put on some short skirts, and wear some high heels, which wasn't really me. And when I said it to my manager, he said, "Oh, I think you should just shave your head." So, I went straightaway across the road in London to this little Greek barber, and it was just a young man there, and he didn't want to do it, he was like ringing his dad and everything and beseeching me not to do it. And then after we did it, it was like the "Nothing Compares 2 U" video. Just one little tear went down his face. He was so upset.

ANA NAVARRO-CÁRDENAS: Sinéad, you know, I live in a pop-culture bubble; I know nothing. But I do know every line and lyric to your "Nothing Compares 2 U" song. And it's still one of the most iconic songs that has spanned several generations. The original song was written by Prince. And in the book, you tell a harrowing story of meeting him for the first time on a night that you say ended in terror. What happened?

O'CONNOR: Oh, we had a disagreement and it got a bit physical between the two of us. It was quite scary for me because I was young and I didn't really know where I was. So, I think that, again, in terms of writing, or quality of writing in the book, the Prince chapter is probably the best chapter in the book because I tried to make it amusing and it is also quite frightening. But yeah, we just, you know, I guess, he

took me to the house, or he got me to go to his house, and
he started telling me that I mustn't swear in my interviews,
and I must talk like this and talk like that, and of course, I
told him, being Irish, how he could take a long walk down
a short pier. And, uh, that didn't go down very well. It all
descended from there . . .

SARA HAINES: Well, Sinéad, in 1992 at the height of your
success, you famously ripped up a photo of Pope John Paul
II on *Saturday Night Live* as a protest to child sex abuse in
the Catholic Church. After that you were booed at concerts,
and your albums were crushed by a steamroller in the street.
Many people believe this ruined your career. But you believe
it did the opposite. Why?

O'CONNOR: Well, you know, speaking of the steamroller-
ing, it was kind of cool because in those days, you probably
remember, the rappers, they used to get Parental Advisory
stickers, and the rest of us used to be jealous. We'd be like,
"Geez, how can we get a Parental Advisory sticker? You're
just not cool if you don't have one." So, getting your albums
steamrollered, that's pretty cool, that's the equivalent of getting ten thousand Parental Advisory stickers. And it's one of
my favorite photos. But, um, that was kind of cool, to be fair.
But, I guess, I am somebody who grew up in the seventies.
My godfathers musically, spiritually, artistically, were Bob
Dylan, John Lennon, and, particularly, Bob Dylan. Bob was
a person who, you know, was quite embarrassed by fame;
he was a protest singer—maybe you might put it that way,
not really all the time. But he certainly wasn't a pop star. So,

I was like a square peg in a round hole in the pop world. And on both sides the relationship just wasn't working out. I couldn't be what everybody, whether it was media or management or whoever, wanted me to be, and they couldn't be what I wanted them to be. So, it was just an accident that I had a hit record, and I guess I feel that derailed my career in many ways because I wasn't able to be—everybody wanted me to be a pop star, and I felt I was a protest singer: one of the children, one of the millions of children, of Bob Dylan and John Lennon.

SUNNY HOSTIN: I think this book is absolutely fantastic. You clearly are a protest singer, and I hope that everyone does read it. As a former sex crimes prosecutor myself, I think that you are extremely brave in the telling of this book, it's really fantastic.

O'CONNOR: Oh, thank you.

HOSTIN: The first part—you're welcome—the first part of your book is a very personal account of the abuse you say you suffered from your mother until she died in a car accident when you were eighteen. And, in the book, you reveal for the first time how your mother related to that particular photo we discussed of the Pope that you ripped up on *Saturday Night Live*. Can you tell us about that?

O'CONNOR: Yeah, well, I guess it goes back to the first question there, where we're talking about the theocracy in Ireland, which is an unimaginable situation—thanks be to God—for anybody in America. You never—thank God—lived under religious oppression in the way we did in Ireland. The church created the type of people who abused their children in their houses, like my mother did. The protest I made when I tore the picture, it wasn't only about sexual abuse, it was about the rest of us—do you know? The reports have been done about the sexual abuse, and everything, and that's obviously hugely valid, and I've fought for that publicly and privately, but, you know, the rest of us never got mentioned. The picture, to me, symbolized the kind of monsters that Catholicism created by, first of all, beating the crap out of kids in school—forgive my language—then those kids going off and becoming parents themselves and thinking, this is how you raise children. Forcing people to get married after their first kiss—you married the first boyfriend, no contraception, no choice for the women as to whether they wanted to be mothers or not. Bang, bang, bang—babies. It was illegal to work once you got married until 1985 or something, so the church created the circumstances where women were so controlled, man-trolled, that they all, when they went to the doctors depressed and postnatal, they were given Valium. They were all miserably unhappy women. What did they do? Went nuts on Valium: beat every shade of "brown stuff," as [one] might say, out of their children.

BEHAR: It's a fascinating read. And I think, also, that Ireland has come a long way since those days, wouldn't you agree? And probably a lot of it has to do with you. I want to thank you, personally, for the things that you have said in the past and continue to say.

O'CONNOR: Thank you. Thank you.

BEHAR: Thank you very much. Her book *Rememberings* is out now. Pick it up! It sounds fascinating, doesn't it, to you people out there. Come on! Buy it!

SINÉAD MARIE BERNADETTE O'CONNOR (December 8, 1966– July 26, 2023) was a singer, songwriter, and activist. Her debut studio album, *The Lion and the Cobra*, was released in 1987 and achieved international chart success. Her 1990 album, *I Do Not Want What I Haven't Got*, was her biggest commercial success, selling over seven million copies worldwide. Her memoir, *Rememberings* (2021), received broad critical praise, and she was the subject of the documentary *Nothing Compares* (2022).

KRISTIN HERSH cofounded her first band, Throwing Muses, when she was 14 years old; they continue to record and perform. She has released more than 20 albums solo, with Throwing Muses, and with her noise rock band, 50 Foot Wave. She is the author of three memoirs and *The Future of Songwriting* (Melville House, 2024). Hersh lives in New Orleans and New England.

The late **KATE HOLMQUIST** was a features writer and commissioning editor for *The Irish Times*. She authored *A Good Daughter* (1991) and *The Glass Room* (2006), and published pieces in *IMAGE* magazine. She was nominated for a NewsBrands News Analysis award in 2013 and the same year won the Business to Arts award. She died on August 5, 2019, in Dublin.

BARRY EGAN is Chief Feature Writer and columnist for *The Sunday Independent* (Ireland). He has written for various publications and outlets such as *NME*, *Creem*, *U Magazine*, and the *Belfast Telegraph*.

DAVID WILD is an Emmy-winning TV writer and producer. He was a longtime writer and editor for *Rolling Stone*, and he is the author of several best-selling books on music and television. Since 2022, Wild has cohosted the podcast *Naked Lunch* with Phil Rosenthal.

BOB GUCCIONE, JR. is an editor and publisher who founded the magazine *SPIN* in 1985.

DEIRDRE MULROONEY is the author of the book *Irish Moves* (The Liffey Press, 2006) and has contributed to various collections and anthologies on theater and dance over the span of her career. She has written for various publications, including *The Irish Independent*. She has curated performance and visual arts exhibitions, as well as screenings of her films, and produced various radio documentaries.

NICHOLAS JENNINGS is a Canadian music journalist. He was the music critic and feature writer for *Maclean's* magazine, and has written for many outlets, such as *Saturday Night*, *Billboard*, and *The Globe and Mail*. He is the author of several books, including the national bestseller *Lightfoot* (Penguin, 2016).

JODY DENBERG is a veteran of the Austin, Texas, radio airwaves who has interviewed such artists as Paul McCartney, R.E.M., and Joni Mitchell. An accomplished journalist whose work has been published in *The Austin Chronicle*, *Rolling Stone*, and *Texas Monthly*, among others, Denberg is a featured DJ in a permanent radio exhibit in the Rock and Roll Hall of Fame. He lives, and still broadcasts, in Austin.

CHRIS AZZOPARDI is the editorial director of Pride Source Media Group and Q Syndicate, the national LGBTQ+ wire service. He has written for *Vanity Fair, GQ, Billboard, New York Magazine,* and *The New York Times,* among many other publications and outlets. He has interviewed celebrities such as Mariah Carey, Cher, Dolly Parton, and Viola Davis.

JOSEPHINE VICTORIA "JOY" BEHAR is an American comedian, television host, and actress. She cohosts the ABC daytime talk show *The View.* Behar has performed in many theatrical plays, including *The Food Chain* and *The Vagina Monologues.* She is the author of multiple books, including *The Great Gasbag: An A–Z Study Guide to Surviving Trump World* (Harper, 2017).

MEGHAN MCCAIN is an American TV personality, columnist, and author. She is the daughter of the late Arizona senator John McCain and Cindy McCain. She served as a cohost on *The View* from 2017 to 2021. She is a columnist for *The Daily Mail.*

ANA VIOLETA NAVARRO-CÁRDENAS is a political strategist and commentator. She appears on various television programs and news outlets, including *CNN, CNN en Español, ABC News,* and *Telemundo.* She is a cohost of the daytime talk show *The View* and, for her work there, has been nominated for various Emmy Awards.

SARA HILARY HAINES is an American television host and journalist. She has been a cohost of the ABC daytime talk shows *The View* and *Strahan and Sara*, and the host of *The Chase*. She has worked as a correspondent on *Today*, *ABC News*, and *Good Morning America*.

ASUNCIÓN "SUNNY" CUMMINGS HOSTIN is an American lawyer, journalist, author, and television host. Hostin is a cohost on ABC's daytime talk show *The View* as well as the senior legal correspondent and analyst for ABC News. She is the author of the *New York Times* best-selling books *Summer on the Bluffs* (William Morrow, 2021) and *Summer on Sag Harbor* (William Morrow, 2022).

THE LAST INTERVIEW SERIES

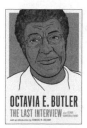

OCTAVIA E. BUTLER:
THE LAST INTERVIEW

$19.99 / $25.99 CAN

978-1-68589-105-3
ebook: 978-1-68589-106-0

bell hooks:
THE LAST INTERVIEW

$18.99 / $24.99 CAN

978-1-68589-079-7
ebook: 978-1-68589-080-3

KURT COBAIN:
THE LAST INTERVIEW

$17.99 / $23.99 CAN

978-1-68589-009-4
ebook: 978-1-68589-010-0

DIEGO MARADONA:
THE LAST INTERVIEW

$17.99 / $23.99 CAN

978-1-61219-973-3
ebook: 978-1-61219-974-0

JOAN DIDION:
THE LAST INTERVIEW

$17.99 / $20.99 OAN

978-1-68589 011-7
ebook: 978-1-68589-012-4

JANET MALCOLM:
THE LAST INTERVIEW

$17.99 / $23.99 CAN

978-1-61219-968-9
ebook: 978-1-68589-012-4

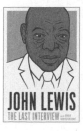

JOHN LEWIS:
THE LAST INTERVIEW

$16.99 / $22.99 CAN

978-1-61219-962-7
ebook: 978-1-61219-963-4

FRIDA KAHLO:
THE LAST INTERVIEW

$16.99 / $22.99 CAN

978-1-61219-875-0
ebook: 978-1-61219-876-7

THE LAST INTERVIEW SERIES

FRED ROGERS:
THE LAST INTERVIEW

$16.99 / $21.99 CAN

978-1-61219-895-8
ebook: 978-1-61219-896-5

TONI MORRISON:
THE LAST INTERVIEW

$16.99 / $22.99 CAN

978-1-61219-873-6
ebook: 978-1-61219-874-3

SHIRLEY CHISHOLM:
THE LAST INTERVIEW

$16.99 / $22.99 CAN

978-1-61219-897-2
ebook: 978-1-61219-898-9

GRAHAM GREENE:
THE LAST INTERVIEW

$16.99 / $22.99 CAN

978-1-61219-814-9
ebook: 978-1-61219-815-6

RUTH BADER GINSBURG:
THE LAST INTERVIEW

$17.99 / $23.99 CAN

978-1-61219-919-1
ebook: 978-1-61219-920-7

URSULA K. LE GUIN:
THE LAST INTERVIEW

$16.99 / $21.99 CAN

978-1-61219-779-1
ebook: 978-1-61219-780-7

JULIA CHILD:
THE LAST INTERVIEW

$16.99 / $22.99 CAN

978-1-61219-733-3
ebook: 978-1-61219-734-0

ROBERTO BOLAÑO:
THE LAST INTERVIEW

$15.95 / $17.95 CAN

978-1-61219-095-2
ebook: 978-1-61219-033-4

THE LAST INTERVIEW SERIES

**KURT VONNEGUT:
THE LAST INTERVIEW**

$15.95 / $17.95 CAN

978-1-61219-090-7
ebook: 978-1-61219-091-4

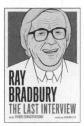

**RAY BRADBURY:
THE LAST INTERVIEW**

$15.95 / $15.95 CAN

978-1-61219-421-9
ebook: 978-1-61219-422-6

**JOHNNY CASH:
THE LAST INTERVIEW**

$16.99 / $22.99 CAN

978-1-61219-893-4
ebook: 978-1-61219-894-1

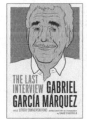

**JAMES BALDWIN:
THE LAST INTERVIEW**

$16.99 / $22.99 CAN

978-1-61219-400-4
ebook: 978-1-61219-401-1

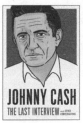

**MARILYN MONROE:
THE LAST INTERVIEW**

$16.99 / $22.99 CAN

978-1-61219-877-4
ebook: 978-1-61219-878-1

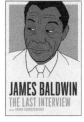

**GABRIEL GARCÍA
MÁRQUEZ: THE LAST
INTERVIEW**

$15.95 / $15.95 CAN

978-1-61219-480-6
ebook: 978-1-61219-481-3

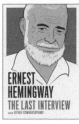

**ERNEST HEMINGWAY:
THE LAST INTERVIEW**

$15.95 / $20.95 CAN

978-1-61219-522-3
ebook: 978-1-61219-523-0

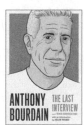

**ANTHONY BOURDAIN:
THE LAST INTERVIEW**

$17.99 / $23.99 CAN

978-1-61219-824-8
ebook: 978-1-61219-825-5

THE LAST INTERVIEW SERIES

PHILIP K. DICK:
THE LAST INTERVIEW

$15.95 / $20.95 CAN

970-1-61219-526-1
ebook: 978-1-61219-527-8

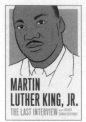

MARTIN LUTHER KING, JR.:
THE LAST INTERVIEW

$15.99 / $21.99 CAN

978-1-61219-616-9
ebook: 978-1-61219-617-6

NORA EPHRON:
THE LAST INTERVIEW

$15.95 / $20.95 CAN

978-1-61219-524-7
ebook: 978-1-61219-525-4

CHRISTOPHER HITCHENS:
THE LAST INTERVIEW

$15.99 / $20.99 CAN

978-1-61219-672-5
ebook: 978-1-61219-673-2

DAVID BOWIE:
THE LAST INTERVIEW

$16.99 / $22.99 CAN

978-1-61219-575-9
ebook: 978-1-61219-576-6

HUNTER S. THOMPSON:
THE LAST INTERVIEW

$15.99 / $20.99 CAN

978-1-61219-693-0
ebook: 978-1-61219-694-7

BILLIE HOLIDAY:
THE LAST INTERVIEW

$16.99 / $22.99 CAN

978-1-61219-674-9
ebook: 978-1-61219-675-6

KATHY ACKER:
THE LAST INTERVIEW

$16.99 / $21.99 CAN

978-1-61219-731-9
ebook: 978-1-61219-732-6